Test Bank to Accompany
BREALEY • MYERS

PRINCIPLES OF CORPORATE FINANCE

FIFTH EDITION

PHILIP R. PERRY
State University of New York at Buffalo

Boston, Massachusetts   Burr Ridge, Illinois   Dubuque, Iowa
Madison, Wisconsin   New York, New York   San Francisco, California   St. Louis, Missouri

McGraw-Hill

A Division of The *McGraw-Hill* Companies

Test Bank to Accompany
PRINCIPLES OF CORPORATE FINANCE Fifth Edition

Copyright © 1996 by The McGraw-Hill Companies, Inc. All rights reserved.
Printed in the United States of America. The contents or parts
thereof may be reproduced for use with
PRINCIPLES OF CORPORATE FINANCE Fifth Editon
by Richard A. Brealey and Stewart C. Myers
provided such reproductions bear copyright notice, but may not
be reproduced in any form for any other purpose without
permission of the publisher.

ISBN 0-07-007419-4

234567890 BKM BKM 90987

PREFACE

This *Test Bank* has been designed for teachers using the fifth edition of *Principles of Corporate Finance*. Questions are arranged by chapter, and include multiple choice questions, true-false questions and essay questions. For the multiple choice questions, the correct answer is marked in the margin by an asterisk (*); please note that for some of these there is more than one correct answer. The correct answer to the true-false questions is indicated in the margin by a T(rue) or an F(alse). The answers to essay questions are in the form of the key points and issues that a complete answer must address.

I have tried to eliminate ambiguities and mistakes, but some undoubtedly remain. If you find something that should be changed, or have any suggestions for improvement of the *Test Bank*, please let me know.

Professor Philip R. Perry
338 Jacobs Center
State University of New York at Buffalo
Buffalo, New York 14260

Chapter 1 - Multiple Choice Questions

1. The financial manager must understand
   a. The firm's operations.
   b. The behavior of capital markets.
 * c. Both of the above.

2. Ultimately financial managers must answer to the firm's
 * a. Shareholders.
   b. Chief executive officer (CEO).
   c. Board of directors.

3. When the firm issues a security to raise cash, it
   a. Sells a real asset.
   b. Sells an intangible asset.
 * c. Sells a financial asset.

4. In large firms, the chief financial officer is likely to
   a. Concentrate on achieving an efficient allocation of funds within the firm.
   b. Concentrate on the firm's relationship with investors in capital markets.
 * c. Supervise other officers taking responsibility for the tasks noted in (a) and (b).

5. Capital budgeting is the choice of
 * a. The real assets the firm will purchase.
   b. The securities the firm will issue.
   c. The firm's overall financial plan.

6. The treasurer usually oversees
 * a. Cash management.
   b. Preparation of financial statements.
   c. Custody of records.
 * d. Pension management.
 * e. Obtaining financing.

7. The controller is usually responsible for
   a. Dividend disbursement.
 * b. Accounting.
 * c. Taxes.
   d. Banking relationships.
 * e. Payroll.

1

8. Sole proprietorships is an organizational form in which
   a. The number of partners is small.
* b. There are no partners.
   c. There is limited liability.

9. In a corporation, the articles of incorporation set out
   a. The purpose of the business.
   b. How many shares can be issued.
   c. The number of directors to be appointed.
* d. All of the above.

10. The organizational form which gives the owner(s) limited liability is the
* a. Corporation.
   b. Partnership.
   c. Sole proprietorship.

11. A corporation which is closely held
   a. Has shares which are widely traded.
   b. Has shares which are owned by a large number of people.
   c. Has shares which are owned by a small number of people.
   d. Has shares which are not widely traded.
* e. C and d.

Chapter 1 - True-False Questions

F 1. Companies invest in a variety of real assets. These include tangible assets, such as management contracts and patents, and intangible assets, such as plant and machinery.

F 2. The financial manager is primarily concerned with achieving efficient use of capital in the firm's operations.

T 3. Financial decisions often have uncertain payoffs extending far into the future.

T 4. In large firms, there is usually a financial vice president who oversees both the treasurer's and controller's work.

F 5. The controller's responsibilities include banking relations and cash management.

F 6. The treasurer is usually responsible for preparation of financial statements.

T 7. The financial manager has two broad responsibilities: what investments the firm should make, and how it should pay for those investments.

F 8. Successful investments are those that enable the firm to maintain its value.

T 9. In a partnership, partners pay personal income tax on their share of the profits.

F 10. Partners in partnerships have limited liability.

T 11. Shareholders in corporations have limited liability.

T 12. Corporations pay tax on their profits and shareholders pay tax on any dividends received, so in effect corporate profits are taxed twice.

F 13. One distinctive feature of a corporation is that there is no separation of ownership and control.

Chapter 1 - Essay Questions

1. Discuss the role of the financial manager.

Answer

    Treasurer - responsible for obtaining financing, managing cash and banking relationships, and making sure the firm meets its obligations to holders of its securities.

    Controller - responsible for accounting functions, payroll, budgets, and taxes.

    Chief Financial Officer - supervises the treasurer and the controller in a large corporation and is involved in corporate planning and capital budgeting.

2. Discuss the primary characteristics of the three main types of ways to organize a business.

Answer

    Sole proprietorship - no partners or stockholders; unlimited liability.

    Partnerships - partners pay personal income tax on their share of the firm's profits; unlimited liability.

    Corporations - distinct legal entity; based on articles of incorporation; limited liability; separation of ownership and control; stockholders elect a board of directors; profits are taxed as are dividends to shareholders.

Chapter 2 - Multiple Choice Questions

1. Other things equal, what happens to a project's NPV if the opportunity cost of capital increases?
    a. It rises.
    * b. It falls.
    c. It could either rise or fall.

2. If NPV is positive,
    * a. The investment return exceeds the opportunity cost of capital.
    b. The investment return is equal to the opportunity cost of capital.
    c. The investment return is less than the opportunity cost of capital.

3. If the one-year discount factor is .75, what is the opportunity cost of capital?
    a. 25 percent.
    * b. 33 percent.
    c. 75 percent.

4. If an investment has cash flows of C_0 and C_1, what is the return on the investment? C_0 is an outflow, and therefore negative; C_1 is an inflow, and hence is positive.

    a. C_1 / C_0

    * b. $(C_1 + C_0) / (-C_0)$

    c. $(C_1 - C_0) / C_0$

5. If the present value of $220 paid at the end of Year 1 is $180, what is the one-year discount factor?
    a. .22
    * b. .82
    c. 1.2

6. If the one-year discount factor is .82, what is the present value of $120 received at the end of Year 1?
    a. $83.00
    * b. $98.40
    c. $144.58

7. The risk-free interest rate is 7 percent. Suppose an asset costs $100 and generates a <u>risky</u> cash flow forecasted at $120. You:
    a. Should reject the project.
    b. Should accept the project because its NPV at 7 percent exceeds +7.
    c. Should accept the project because its 20 percent rate of return exceeds the 7 percent cost of capital.
*   d. Can't decide without knowing the expected rate of return on equally risky investments.

8. A diverse group of shareholders will all agree on their company's capital budgeting decisions if:
    a. They can all lend at the same rate.
    b. Their lending rate is less than their borrowing rate.
*   c. They all can lend or borrow at the same rate.

9. Which of the following is a tangible asset?
    a. Common stock.
*   b. Machinery.
    c. Patents.
    d. None of the above.

10. Which of the following is an intangible asset?
    a. Property.
    b. Machinery.
*   c. Patents.
    d. None of the above.

11. To calculate present value, we discount by a rate of return that is known as the:
    a. Opportunity cost of capital.
    b. Hurdle rate.
    c. Discount rate.
*   d. All of the above.
    e. None of the above.

12. If the chance of a slump is 25%, the chance of normal times 50%, and the chance of a boom 25%, what is the expected payoff from an investment which offers the following payoffs?

	Slump	Normal	Boom
	$100	$200	$300

*   a. $200
    b. $300
    c. $600
    d.   None of the above.

13. If the chance of a slump is 40%, the chance of normal times 25%, and the chance of a boom 35%, what is the expected payoff from an investment which offers the following payoffs?

	Slump	Normal	Boom
	$500	$300	$100

    a. $200
    b. $400
    c. $800
*   d.   None of the above.

14. If the chance of a slump is 30%, the chance of normal times 50%, and the chance of a boom 20%, what is the expected payoff from an investment which offers the following payoffs?

	Slump	Normal	Boom
	$200	$200	$400

    a. $800
    b. $560
*   c. $240
    d.   None of the above.

15. The Investment Opportunity Set may be described as a curve which reflects:
*   a.   Declining marginal returns on capital.
    b.   Constant marginal returns on capital.
    c.   Increasing marginal returns on capital.
    d.   Constant average cost of capital.
    e.   None of the above.

16. The appropriate goal of a corporation is to:
    a. Maximize profits.
    b. Earn the highest return possible on investments.
    c. Maximize market share.
    d. All of the above.
    * e. None of the above.

17. One of the most important assets of a corporation is:
    * a. Its reputation.
    b. Its patents.
    c. Its products.
    d. None of the above.

18. Managers are monitored by:
    a. The board of directors.
    b. Commercial banks that have loans outstanding to the firm.
    c. Wall Street analysts.
    * d. All of the above.

19. Which of the following statements is correct?
    a. Misers will always choose to borrow.
    * b. The capital market removes the obligation to match consumption and cash flow.
    c. Prodigals will always choose to borrow.
    d. None of the above.

20. The opportunity cost of capital for a project is the:
    a. Expected rate of return on government securities having the same maturity as the project.
    b. Expected rate of return on a well-diversified portfolio of common stocks.
    * c. Expected rate of return demanded by investors in securities subject to the same risks as the project.
    d. None of the above.

Chapter 2 - True-False Questions

T   1.   A dollar today is worth more than a dollar tomorrow because the dollar today can be invested and will start earning interest immediately.

T   2.   The present value of a delayed payoff may be found by multiplying by the appropriate discount factor.

F   3.   The discount factor is expressed as one plus a rate of return. The rate of return is the reward that investors demand for accepting delayed payment.

T   4.   To calculate present value, we discount expected future payoffs by the rate of return offered by comparable investment alternatives. This rate of return is called the opportunity cost of capital.

T   5.   Net present value is found by subtracting the required investment from present value.

F   6.   Investments increase wealth if they have a positive present value.

T   7.   The return on capital invested is equal to the profit as a proportion of the initial outlay.

F   8.   The opportunity cost of capital is the rate the firm would pay to borrow additional money.

F   9.   The opportunity cost of capital is higher for safe assets than for risky ones.

F   10. There are two equivalent decision rules for capital investment: (1) "Accept investments that have positive net present values," and (2) "Accept investments that offer rates of return below their opportunity costs of capital."

F   11. Managers cannot act in the best interests of their shareholders unless they know when the shareholders want to spend their money and what risks they are prepared to assume.

T   12. The fundamental assumption behind the net present value rule is that there exists a perfectly competitive capital market which individuals can use to adjust the risk and time pattern of their consumption.

F   13. To calculate present value, we discount expected future payoffs by the rate of return offered by comparable investment alternatives. This rate of return is called the risk-free rate of return.

T   14.   A contract is an example of an intangible asset.

F   15.   The Investment Opportunity Set has a characteristic shape which reflects increasing marginal returns on investment.

T   16.   Strictly speaking, in a world with different rates for borrowing and lending, the net present value rule does not apply.

T   17.   Under perfect market conditions, the individual's preferences for current versus consumption are irrelevant: Everyone agrees that "maximize net present value" is best.

F   18.   Under perfect market conditions, managers must know their stockholders' preferences before they can make investment decisions.

F   19.   The goal of the corporation should be to maximize profits.

T   20.   The firm's reputation is one of its most important assets.

Chapter 2 - Essay Questions

1. Many managers argue that the goal of the firm is to maximize profits. Do you agree?

Answer

The goal of the firm should be to maximize the wealth of its owners, i.e., to maximize shareholder wealth. Maximizing profits does not necessarily accomplish this goal:
- Which year's profits are to be maximized is ambiguous.
- Profits may increase as the result of accepting a negative net present value project.
- Profits are dependent upon choice of accounting method, which may or may not have any effect on cash flow.

2. Explain why "maximize shareholder wealth" is the appropriate goal of the firm.

Answer

Under perfect market conditions, all can borrow or lend at the same rate of interest. This implies that differences in consumption patterns can be adjusted in the capital markets, i.e., investors do not need to match the cash flow of their investments to their consumption plans. Given this, all investors will agree that they are better off if the firm maximizes the present value of their wealth, i.e., maximizes shareholder wealth. Because all investors in the firm (i.e., the firm's owners) want this, it becomes the goal of the firm.

Chapter 3 - Multiple Choice Questions

1. What is the relationship between the 2-year discount factor and the 1-year discount factor?
   * a. DF_2 is never more than DF_1.
   b. DF_2 is never less than DF_1.
   c. DF_2 could be either more or less than DF_1.
   d. DF_2 is equal to DF_1.

2. If the 3-year rate of interest is 12 percent per year, what is the 3-year discount factor?
   * a. .712
   b. 1.405
   c. 2.4021
   d. .893

3. If the 3-year discount factor is .800 what is the rate of interest?
   a. Less than 7 percent.
   * b. More than 7 percent.
   c. 7 percent.

4. If the 2-year discount factor is .842 and the 3-year discount factor is .722, what is the present value of a 3-year annuity of $1 a year?
   a. $.070
   b. $1.614
   c. $2.531
   * d. Can't say.

5. If the 3-year annuity factor is 2.361 and the 2-year annuity factor is 1.668, what is the present value of $1 received in year 3?
   * a. $.693
   b. $4.029
   c. $3.938
   d. Can't say.

6. Consider the following two questions: "What is the present value of $100 to be received in 10 years if the cost of capital is 17 percent?" and "How much would I have to invest now in order to receive $100 after 10 years, given an interest rate of 17 percent?" The answers to these two questions are:
   * a. The same.
   b. Different.
   c. Can't say.

7. Michael Parsnip has just taken out a $100,000 mortgage at an interest rate of 8 percent. If the mortgage calls for 20 equal annual payments, what is the amount of each payment?
   a. $5,000
   b. $7,924
 * c. $10,185
   d. $21,455

8. Michael Parsnip has just taken out a $100,000 mortgage at an interest rate of 8 percent. What is the value of the mortgage after the payment of the second annual installment?
   a. $79,630
   b. $85,734
   c. $90,000
 * d. $95,454

9. The annual subscription to a magazine is $50 and is expected to increase by 5 percent a year. A life subscription is $500 and the discount rate is 12 percent. In order to justify taking out a life subscription, what is your minimum life expectancy?
   a. 5 years.
   b. 10 years.
 * c. 15 years.
   d. 20 years.

10. You own an office building. A fair rent for this building next year would be $100,000, and you expect that thereafter rents will increase indefinitely by 5 percent a year. Somebody has expressed an interest in renting the building at a fixed annual rent for 20 years. If the cost of capital is 15 percent, what would be a fair rental for 20 years?
    a. About $200,000.
    b. About $180,000.
    c. About $150,000.
 * d. About $140,000.

11. How much is $100 worth at the end of 4 years if invested at a continuously compounded rate of 10 percent a year?
    a. $143.60
    b. $146.40
 * c. $149.20
    d. $317.00

12. Suppose you have just won the lottery and must choose one of the following (guaranteed) payoffs. Which one would you choose? The interest rate is 7%; ignore tax consequences.
    a. $100,000 paid today.
    b. $140,000 paid five years from today.
    c. $50,000 paid one year from today and $68,000 paid four years from today.
*   d. $14,000 paid per year for ten years, with the first year's payment made today.

13. Suppose you have just won the lottery and must choose one of the following (guaranteed) payoffs. Which one would you choose? The interest rate is 10%; ignore tax consequences.
    a. $500,000 paid today.
*   b. $160,000 paid at the beginning of each year (first payment today) for a total of four years.
    c. Annual payments of $57,000 forever, with the first payment two years from today.
*   d. Annual payments forever, growing at 6% per year; the first payment of $22,000 is one year from today.

14. Suppose you invested $1,000 at a nominal rate of 9% for one year and the rate of inflation was 5%. What was the real rate of return on this investment?
    a. 9.0%
    b. 5.0%
    c. 4.0%
*   d. 3.8%

15. Suppose you invested $10,000 for ten years at a nominal rate of 7% per year. If the annual rate of inflation was 3%, what was the real value of your investment at the end of the ten years?
    a. $19,671
    b. $14,802
*   c. $14,637
    d. $13,439

16. Suppose you invested $20,000 at a nominal rate of 15% for one year and the rate of inflation was 6%. What was the real rate of return on this investment?
    a. 6.0%
*   b. 8.5%
    c. 15.0%
    d. 20.0%

17. A 10 percent 8-year bond yields 12 percent. Assuming annual coupon payments, what is the price?
    a.   49.68 percent of par.
*   b.   90.06 percent of par.
    c.   110.66 percent of par.
    d.   120.00 percent of par.

18. Consider a bond with a face value of $1,000, a coupon rate of 6 percent (with annual coupon payments), and a yield of 6 percent. The price of the bond is:
    a.   Less than $1,000.
*   b.   Equal to $1,000.
    c.   Greater than $1,000.
    d.   Cannot say: It depends on the bond's maturity.

19. Consider a 5-year bond with a face value of $1,000, a coupon rate of 6 percent (with semiannual coupon payments), and a yield of 8 percent. The price of the bond is:
    a. $243.33
    b. $800.00
*   c. $918.89
    d. $1,085.30

20. Holding the coupon rate and face value constant, as the yield on a bond increases, the price of the bond will:
*   a.   Fall.
    b.   Remain unchanged.
    c.   Increase.
    d.   Cannot say: It depends on the bond's maturity.

21. One of the following debt securities has a yield of 9.5 percent. Which one? Assume annual compounding.
    a.   A 15-year bond selling at 90 percent of par. The coupon is 9.5 percent.
*   b.   A 5-year note selling at 105.76 percent of par. The coupon is 11 percent.
    c.   A perpetuity with a coupon of 9 percent is selling at 86 percent of par.
    d.   A 1-year note selling at 95 percent of par. The coupon rate is 5 percent.

Chapter 3 - True-False Questions

F   1. The ten-year discount factor must be greater than the nine-year discount factor.

F   2. If the ten-year rate of interest is less than the nine-year rate, there must be a money machine.

T   3. If the term structure of interest rates is flat, the nine-year interest rate equals the ten-year interest rate.

T   4. The return on a perpetuity is equal to the cash flow divided by the price.

F   5. The present value of a perpetuity is equal to the cash flow multiplied by the opportunity cost of capital.

F   6. If the cash flow from an investment increases indefinitely at a steady rate g, then the present value of the investment is given by: $C_1 / (r + g)$.

T   7. An equal-payment house mortgage and an installment credit agreement are examples of annuities.

T   8. The value of a five-year annuity is equal to the difference between the present value of two perpetuities. One makes its first payment in year 1, the other makes its first payment in year 6.

F   9. When money is invested at simple interest, each interest payment is reinvested to earn more interest in subsequent periods.

T   10. If interest compounds continuously, your investment grows more rapidly than if interest compounds annually.

F   11. If money is invested in a bank at compound interest, the percentage rate of growth of the balance increases as time passes.

T   12. If money is invested in a bank at simple interest, the percentage rate of increase of the bank balance decreases as time passes.

F   13. The present value of a perpetuity (with cash flow C) at the continuously compounded rate r is given by: C / e^r.

T 14. The present value of a 10-year annuity at the continuously compounded rate r is given by:

$$(C/r)\left[1 - (1/e^{10r})\right]$$

T 15. If the term structure of interest rates is flat, then the interest rate is the same regardless of the date of the cash flow.

F 16. A security that has no maturity date but that pays a fixed income for each year is called an annuity.

T 17. A security that pays a fixed sum each year for a specified number of years is called an annuity.

F 18. The distinction between an investment at compound interest and an investment at simple interest is that an investment at simple interest provides the opportunity to earn interest on interest while an investment at compound interest does not.

F 19. Discounting is a process involving simple interest.

T 20. The following equation is correct:

$$1 + r_{nominal} = (1 + r_{real})(1 + \text{inflation rate})$$

T 21. Any bond can be valued as a package of an annuity (the coupon payments) and a single payment (the principal).

F 22. In the U.S. most bonds make coupon payments annually.

Chapter 3 - Essay Questions

1. Discuss why a dollar tomorrow cannot be worth less than a dollar the day after tomorrow.

Answer
      This question goes to the heart of how financial markets operate, and to some extent foreshadows the material on efficient markets. The key is to recognize that, if a dollar today were indeed worth less than a dollar the day after tomorrow, it would be possible to earn a very large amount of money. This is only possible, of course, if someone else is losing a very large amount of money; while this may be possible in the short run (bookies, for example, who misquote betting odds so that some combination of bets always wins), it cannot exist in equilibrium because the source of money is quickly exhausted.

2. Discuss the importance of taking inflation into account when making financial decisions. Is it easy or hard to incorporate inflation into financial calculations?

Answer
      Financial decisions involve money and inflation reduces the purchasing power of money, and so inflation is a critical element of financial decisions. In a mechanistic sense it is easy to incorporate inflation; the key problem is knowing the rate of inflation to use.

Chapter 4 - Multiple Choice Questions

1. The sale of shares to raise new capital takes place in the:
   * a. Primary market.
   b. Secondary market.
   c. Over-the-counter market.

2. $DIV_1 = \$10$, $DIV_2 = \$20$, $P_0 = \$60$ and $r = .12$. What is P_2?
   * a. $44.06
   b. $49.35
   c. $84.30

3. Company A's dividends are expected to grow at a constant rate of $g = .04$. $DIV_1 = \$50$ and $r = .08$. What is the current price?
   a. $ 400
   b. $ 625
   * c. $1,250

4. Company B's dividends are expected to grow at a constant rate of g. $P_0 = \$40$, $DIV_1 = \$2$, and $r = .10$. What is g?
   * a. .05
   b. .10
   c. .15

5. Company C's dividends are expected to grow at a constant rate of g. It has just paid a dividend DIV_0. What is the current price?

   a. $P_0 = \dfrac{DIV_0 (1 + r)}{r - g}$

   * b. $P_0 = \dfrac{DIV_0 (1 + g)}{r - g}$

   c. $P_0 = \dfrac{DIV_0}{r - g}$

   d. $P_0 = \dfrac{DIV_0 (1 + g)}{r + g}$

6. What is the relationship between the earnings-price ratio and the market capitalization rate?
* a. E/P underestimates r if the present value of growth opportunities is positive.
   b. E/P overestimates r if the present value of growth opportunities is positive.
   c. There is no relationship between the earnings-price ratio and the market capitalization rate.

7. The stock price equals the capitalized value of average earnings under a no-growth policy, plus:
   a. The dividend yield.
   b. The earnings per share.
* c. The present value of growth opportunities.

8. $DIV_1 = \$10$, $P_1 = \$60$, $r = .15$. What is the current price?
   a. $43.48
   b. $52.17
* c. $60.87

9. A firm's book return on equity is 16 percent, and it reinvests 50 percent of its earnings. How fast will its earnings and assets grow?
   a. 16 percent per year.
* b. 8 percent per year.
   c. 20 percent per year.
   d. 50 percent per year.

10. A firm pays a dividend of $1, which is expected to grow at 12 percent. What is the stock price if the discount rate is 9 percent?
    a. $133.
    b. Infinite.
* c. Can't answer without knowing how long growth will continue.

11. Suppose $EPS_1 = 2.20$, $r = .11$, and $P_0 = 35$.
* a. Investors expect the firm to earn more than 11 percent on growth investments.
    b. Investors expect the firm to grow at a rate of at least 11 percent per year.
* c. Investors expect the firm to have positive-NPV investment opportunities.

12. Consider a constant growth company. If the plowback ratio is 30% and the return on equity (ROE) is 15%, the expected growth rate is:
* a. 4.5%
  b. 10.5%
  c. 70.0%

13. A growth stock is one for which:
   a. Earnings per share is expected to constantly increase.
* b. PVGO is a significant fraction of its current share price.
   c. Dividends are expected to constantly increase.

14. Growth stocks sell at high price-earnings (P/E) ratios because:
   a. This is false: growth stocks do not sell at high P/E ratios.
   b. Investors are willing to pay a high price for stocks with temporarily depressed earnings.
* c. Investors are willing to pay now for expected superior returns on company investments that have not yet been made.

15. Free cash flow is defined as:
* a. Revenue - costs - investments
   b. Revenue - costs + investments
   c. Revenue + costs - investments
   d. Revenue + costs + investments

16. The price of a stock is the present value of:
   a. Expected future dividends.
   b. Expected free cash flow.
* c. Both (a) and (b).
   d. None of the above.

17. A firm's price-earnings (P/E) ratio is affected by the firm's choice of:
   a. Inventory valuation method.
   b. Whether to expense or capitalize research and development.
* c. Both (a) and (b).
   d. None of the above.

18. A firm's present value of growth opportunities (PVGO) will be equal to zero if:
    a. The firm currently pays no dividends.
  * b. The firm's competitors are just as smart and efficient as the firm itself.
    c. Earnings per share (EPS) this year are equal to last year's EPS.
    d. None of the above.

19. When attempting to value a business, one key component is the horizon value. It is usually best to estimate this horizon value:
    a. Using the discounted cash flow formula, assuming a constant rate of growth.
    b. Using a price-earnings (P/E) ratio approach.
    c. Using a market-book ratio approach.
  * d. Using all of the above methods.

20. A company's current share price is $50, earnings per share next year (i.e., EPS_1) is expected to be $3.00, and the market capitalization rate is 15%. This company's ratio of the present value of growth opportunities (PVGO) to share price is:
  * a. .60
    b. .40
    c. .20
    d. .67

Chapter 4 - True-False Questions

F   1. The sale of new shares to raise additional capital occurs in the secondary market.

F   2. The New York Stock Exchange is the only stock market in the United States.

T   3. On the New York Stock Exchange, trading in each stock is the responsibility of a specialist.

F   4. Shareholders receive cash from the company in the form of dividends and capital gains.

T   5. The return that is expected by investors from a common stock is often called its market capitalization rate.

T   6. At each point in time, all securities in an equivalent-risk class are priced to offer the same expected return.

F   7. The rate of return expected from a share is equal to the expected dividend per share plus the expected price, all divided by the price at the end of the year.

T   8. If dividends are expected to grow indefinitely at a steady rate, the market capitalization rate equals the dividend yield plus the expected rate of growth in dividends.

F   9. The plowback ratio equals one plus the payout ratio.

F   10. The constant-growth formula for stock valuation is best applied to firms with high current rates of growth.

F   11. The constant growth formula may be used to test whether the market has correctly priced a common stock.

T   12. The market capitalization rate for firms whose dividends and earnings are not expected to grow at all is the dividend yield.

F   13. As long as the firm has opportunities to invest money to earn a return above the return required by investors, the market capitalization rate is equal to the price-earnings multiple.

F   14. The earnings yield will overestimate the market capitalization rate if PVGO is positive.

F   15. A share's value is equal to the discounted stream of earnings per share.

T   16. A share's value is equal to the discounted stream of free cash flow per share.

T   17. If return on equity is constant, the rate of growth in dividends and earnings is:
$$g = (1 - \text{payout ratio}) \cdot ROE$$

F   18. There is a strong relationship between a stock's price-earnings (P/E) ratio and its capitalization rate.

T   19. In the 1970s, some utilities were forced to continue growing (and investing) even though allowed rates of return were less than the opportunity cost of capital. In these circumstances, the present value of growth opportunities was negative.

F   20. Discounted cash flow is often used to value companies or businesses. In this case, the relevant formula is:

$$PV = \sum_{t=1}^{H} \frac{\text{Net Earnings}}{(1+r)^t} + \frac{PV_H}{(1+r)^H}$$

where PV_H = the company's horizon value.

F   21. Discounted cash flow cannot be used to value ongoing businesses with negative cash flows - i.e., businesses absorbing more cash than they are generating.

Chapter 4 - Essay Questions

1. Discuss using the discounted cash flow formula to estimate a company's capitalization rate (i.e., the fair rate of return).

Answer
The usual assumption is that the stock has a constant growth rate (g), and so this approach is most applicable to companies for which this is reasonable, i.e., those that are mature and stable. The main difficulty is in estimating the growth rate; small changes in g can translate into big differences in estimates of the capitalization rate. In general, any single estimate is insufficient; one should attempt to gather similar companies, estimate r for each, and use some average measure.

2. Discuss the price-earnings (P/E) ratio.

Answer
The P/E ratio is a widely used financial indicator, but is also one which is somewhat ambiguous. The primary difficulty is that it is usually measured with current earnings, while the market price is based on future prospects. In general, a high P/E ratio indicates that investors think a company has good growth prospects, that its earnings are relatively safe and deserve a low capitalization rate, or possibly both. The P/E ratio can also be helpful in evaluating stocks. It is important to remember, however, that some accounting choices made by the firm will affect earnings per share (e.g., inventory valuation method) and hence will affect the P/E ratio.

3. Discuss the problems inherent in the valuation of a business, as well as how these problems might be addressed.

Answer
The key problems are estimating future cash flow for the next several years and estimating the horizon value. The latter is particularly difficult and is frequently a significant proportion of the total estimated value of the company. In general, one should use several approaches, perhaps with more weight given to some than others; the final price will then be the result of negotiations between the buyer and the seller. The usual approaches to estimating the horizon value are to use the discounted cash flow formula, assuming a constant rate of growth; to use the price-earnings (P/E) ratio; and to use the market-book ratio.

Chapter 5 - Multiple Choice Questions

1. Projects A and B have the following cash flows:

	t=0	t=1	t=2	t=3	t=4
A	-100	+40	+30	+30	+30
B	-80	+40	+40	0	0

   If a company uses the payback rule with a cutoff period of 2 years, which projects would it accept?
       a. Project A.
   *   b. Project B.
       c. Both.
       d. Neither.

2. Projects A and B have the following cash flows:

	t=0	t=1	t=2	t=3	t=4
A	-180	+100	+80	+80	+50
B	-200	+70	+70	+60	+60

   If a company uses the payback rule with a cutoff period of 2 years, which projects would it accept?
   *   a. Project A.
       b. Project B.
       c. Both.
       d. Neither.

3. If the firm decides to depreciate a large portion of an investment in the first year, what is the effect on the investment's average return on book?
       a. It will be increased.
       b. It will be reduced.
   *   c. Can't say without knowing whether the investment is profitable.

4. The opportunity cost of capital is 12 percent. Projects A and B both cost $1,000 and both have an NPV of $42. A has an IRR of 14 percent and B of 15 percent. What is the IRR on the incremental cash flows?
       a. 0 percent.
   *   b. 12 percent.
       c. 16 percent.
       d. Need more information to solve.

5. A project has the following cash flows:

t=0	t=1	t=2	t=3
-100	+35	+40	+60

What is the IRR (to the nearest percent)?
*   a. 15 percent.
    b. 20 percent.
    c. 25 percent.
    d. None of the above.

6. A project has the following cash flows and IRR:

t=0	t=1	t=2	t=3	IRR
+100	-42	-60	-40	18%

If the opportunity cost of capital is less than 18 percent, what should the company do?
    a. Accept the project.
*   b. Reject the project.
    c. Can't tell from the data given.

7. You must undertake one of the following two mutually exclusive projects:

	t=0	t=1	t=2
A	-300	+500	0
B	-200	+200	+200

Under what conditions should B be preferred to A?
    a. If the cost of capital is less than 0 or greater than 50 percent.
    b. If the cost of capital is between 0 and 50 percent.
*   c. If the cost of capital is less than 0 or greater than 100 percent.
    d. Need more information to solve.

8. Pitfalls of the Internal Rate of Return (IRR) rule include:
    a. Confusion between lending and borrowing.
    b. Multiple rates of return.
    c. Mutually exclusive projects.
*   d. All of the above.
    e. None of the above.

9. Which of the following criteria, correctly used, give(s) the same accept/reject decisions as NPV?
    a. Payback.
    b. Discounted payback.
    c. Average return on book.
*   d. Internal rate of return.
    e. None of the above.

10. Which of the following statements is/are correct?
*   a. A project can have as many IRRs as there are changes in sign in its cash flow stream.
    b. A project has at least as many IRRs as there are changes in sign in its cash flow stream.
    c. All projects have at least one IRR.
*   d. Some projects have no meaningful IRR.

11. A company has a limit of $200 million to invest and has the following possible investment opportunities. The cost of capital is 8%.

Project	Investment, Millions	NPV, Millions	IRR, Percent
A	100	140	15
B	20	20	15
C	50	65	43
D	50	-10	5
E	150	30	10
F	40	32	50
G	20	18	30

Given the limited amount of investment, what is the maximum NPV that the company can obtain?
    a. $200 million.
*   b. $243 million.
    c. $283 million.
    d. Need more information to solve.

12. Consider the following project and its associated cash flows; the appropriate discount rate is 20%:

	t=0	t=1	t=2	t=3	t=4
Project	-$50,000	$20,000	$22,000	$24,000	$21,000

The Internal Rate of Return (to the nearest percent) for the project is:
*   a. 26% and the project should be accepted.
    b. 26% and the project should not be accepted.
    c. 18% and the project should be accepted.
    d. 18% and the project should not be accepted.
    e. None of the above.

13. A company has a limit of $20 million to invest and has the following possible investment opportunities. The cost of capital is 11%.

Project	Investment, Millions	NPV, Millions	IRR, Percent
A	6.0	1.32	17.2
B	4.0	-.08	10.7
C	5.0	.86	16.6
D	2.0	.28	12.1
E	2.0	.14	11.8
F	7.0	1.26	18.0
G	8.0	.96	13.5

Given the limited amount of investment, what is the maximum NPV that the company can obtain?
* a. $3.72 million.
  b. $4.74 million.
  c. $4.82 million.
  d. None of the above.

14. Your company is considering three different projects (X, Y, and Z). Cash flows estimates have been made and the projects analyzed (see table below). The appropriate rate of return is 10%, and each project costs $10 (all dollar amounts are in millions). Unfortunately, the capital allocation committee can authorize only one of these projects.

	Payback	(Net) Present Value	Internal Rate of Return
Proj. X	1.0 yr	.7	17.1%
Proj. Y	3.0 yr	11.6	39.0%
Proj. Z	1.2 yr	6.0	46.1%

What should the capital allocation committee recommend?

   a. Accept Project X, reject Projects Y and Z.
* b. Accept Project Y, reject Projects X and Z.
   c. Accept Project Z, reject Projects X and Y.
   d. Reject all three projects.

15. Consider the following project and its associated cash flows; the appropriate discount rate is 20%:

	t=0	t=1	t=2	t=3	t=4
Project	-$50,000	$15,000	$20,000	$20,000	$10,000

The Internal Rate of Return (to the nearest percent) for the project is:
- a. 22% and the project should be accepted.
- b. 22% and the project should not be accepted.
- c. 15% and the project should be accepted.
- d. 15% and the project should not be accepted.
- * e. None of the above.

16. Consider the following project and its associated cash flows; the appropriate discount rate is 18%:

	t=0	t=1	t=2	t=3
Project	-$29,000	$20,000	$10,000	$10,000

The Internal Rate of Return (to the nearest percent) for the project is:
- * a. 21% and the project should be accepted.
- b. 21% and the project should not be accepted.
- c. 17% and the project should be accepted.
- d. 17% and the project should not be accepted.
- e. None of the above.

17. Consider the following mutually exclusive projects and their associated cash flows; the appropriate discount rate is 20%:

	t=0	t=1	t=2	t=3	t=4
Project A	-$50,000	$20,000	$22,000	$24,000	$21,000
Project B	-$30,000	$10,000	$13,000	$15,000	$17,000

You have already calculated the IRRs of the individual projects: for project A, the IRR is 26.1%; for project B, the IRR is 26.6%. The IRR (to the nearest percent) of the incremental cash flows is:
- a. 17% and Project A should be accepted.
- b. 17% and Project B should be accepted.
- * c. 25% and Project A should be accepted.
- d. 25% and Project B should be accepted.
- e. None of the above.

18. Consider the following mutually exclusive projects and their associated cash flows; the appropriate discount rate is 20%:

	t=0	t=1	t=2	t=3	t=4
Project A	-$25,000	$12,000	$10,000	$10,000	$8,000
Project B	-$19,000	$9,000	$8,000	$8,000	$7,000

You have already calculated the IRRs of the individual projects: for project A, the IRR is 23.5%; for project B, the IRR is 27.4%. The IRR (to the nearest percent) of the incremental cash flows is:
    a. 15% and Project A should be accepted.
*   b. 15% and Project B should be accepted.
    c. 27% and Project A should be accepted.
    d. 27% and Project B should be accepted.
    e. None of the above.

19. Consider the following project cash flows; the appropriate discount rate is 20%:

	t=0	t=1	t=2	t=3	t=4
Project A	-$27,000	$18,000	$16,000	$13,000	$12,000

Project A's profitability index is:
    a. 1.46 and Project A should be accepted.
    b. 1.46 and Project A should be rejected.
*   c. .46 and Project A should be accepted.
    d. .46 and Project A should be rejected.

20. Consider the following project cash flows; the appropriate discount rate is 14%:

	t=0	t=1	t=2	t=3	t=4
Project B	-$10,000	$4,000	$3,000	$3,000	$2,000

Project B's profitability index is:
    a. .90 and Project B should be accepted.
    b. .90 and Project B should be rejected.
    c. - .10 and Project B should be accepted.
*   d. - .10 and Project B should be rejected.

Chapter 5 - True-False Questions

T   1. Any investment rule should depend solely on forecasted cash flows and the opportunity cost of capital. It should not be affected by managers' tastes, the choice of accounting method, or the profitability of other independent projects.

F   2. Because present values refer to cash flows that occur at different points in time, they cannot be added.

T   3. Because present values are all measured in terms of today's dollars, you can add them up.

T   4. The payback period of a project is found by counting the number of years it takes before cumulative cash flows equal the initial investment.

T   5. The payback rule gives equal weight to all cash flows before the payback date and no weight at all to subsequent flows.

F   6. The discounted payback rule calculates the payback period and then discounts it at the opportunity cost of capital.

F   7. The average-return-on-book-value rule gives too little weight to distant cash flows.

T   8. The average return on book value depends on which items the accountant treats as capital investments and how rapidly he or she depreciates them.

F   9. The internal rate of return is the rate of discount that makes PV = 0.

T   10. The IRR rule states that companies should accept any project offering an internal rate of return in excess of the cost of capital.

F   11. The internal-rate-of-return rule gives the same answer as the net present value rule whenever the NPV of a project is a smoothly increasing function of the discount rate.

T   12. If the initial cash flow is positive and subsequent ones are negative, one should accept projects whose IRR is <u>lower</u> than the cost of capital.

T   13. There may be as many different internal rates of return for a project as there are changes in the signs of the cash flows.

T   14. In order to use the internal rate of return rule to choose between mutually exclusive projects, it is necessary to calculate the IRR of the incremental cash flows.

F   15. Projects may be ranked using their internal rates of return (IRRs), i.e., the best project has the highest IRR, the second-best project has the second-highest IRR, etc.

F   16. Suppose a company may invest in project A or project B, but not in both. Project A's IRR is less than the opportunity cost of capital. Project B, which is the larger project, should be accepted if the IRR of the incremental cash flows exceeds the cost of capital.

F   17. A company has two attractive projects A and B, each with IRRs exceeding the cost of capital. The firm can safely accept the project with higher IRR, as long as A and B are expected to have the same economic life.

F   18. Project A has an IRR of 16 percent and Project B an IRR of 14 percent. The cost of capital is 8 percent. Unfortunately, the projects are mutually exclusive. The company should choose A as long as A and B require the same investment outlay.

T   19. In order to evaluate a project, a manager should identify financial assets with risks equivalent to the project under consideration, estimate the expected rate of return on these assets, and use this rate as the opportunity cost.

T   20. When capital is rationed, the company should choose that combination of projects that, within the company's resources, gives the highest net present value.

F   21. The profitability index can be used to choose between projects whenever cash available for investment is constrained in more than one period.

T   22. Where there is more than one constraint on the choice of projects, linear programming or integer programming can be used to select the combination of investments that maximizes NPV.

Chapter 5 - Essay Questions

1. Discuss the advantages and disadvantages of the internal rate of return rule.

Answer
Advantages are that (1) it gives the same accept/reject signal as does net present value, and (2) it has great intuitive appeal (people think they understand what an IRR means).

Disadvantages are that (1) projects cannot simply be ranked by IRR (i.e., such a ranking may be inconsistent with a ranking based on net present value), (2) whether we are borrowing or lending affects the interpretation of the IRR, (3) there is a potential for multiple rates of return, and (4) the IRR method may be inappropriate if the yield curve is not flat.

2. Discuss capital rationing.

Answer
There are two types of capital rationing. One is called soft and is when the budget constraint is imposed by the company, usually as a method for controlling managers' behavior. The other is hard and is when the budget constraint is imposed by the capital markets. In either case, capital rationing means the company is giving up some positive net present value projects, and in this sense capital rationing imposes a cost on the firm.

Under capital rationing, the goal should be to select the package of projects that, within the company's resources, gives the highest net present value. If the only resource that is rationed is capital at t=0, the profitability index may be used to rank projects and hence may be used to select the best package of projects.

Chapter 6 - Multiple Choice Questions

1. Which of the following cash flows should be treated as incremental flows when deciding whether to go ahead with production of a new car model?
* a. The consequent reduction in the sales of the company's existing models.
* b. The expenditure on new plant and equipment.
* c. The value of tools that can be transferred from the company's existing plants.
   d. The cost of research and development undertaken on the model during the past 3 years.
   e. The annual depreciation charge.
* f. The reduction in the tax bill resulting from the depreciation charge.
   g. Interest payments.
   h. Dividend payments.
   i. A proportion of head office expenses.
* j. The salvage value of plant and equipment at the end of the project's life.

2. A project has the following expected real cash flows:

t=0	t=1	t=2	t=3
-80	+30	+20	+10

The expected inflation rate is 5 percent a year, and the real cost of capital is 8 percent a year. What is the NPV?
   a. -17.10
* b. -27.14
   c. -31.13

3. A machine lasts 3 years and has the following costs:

t=0	t=1	t=2	t=3
$30,000	$8,000	$8,000	$8,000

If the cost of capital is 8 percent, what is the present value of the costs of operating a series of such machines in perpetuity?
   a. $50,617
* b. $245,518
   c. $632,710

4. Which of the following statements is/are wrong?
   a. It is standard practice to discount after-tax cash flows at the opportunity cost of capital.
 * b. However, you can get the same NPV by using pre-tax cash flows and a pre-tax rate. The pre-tax rate is $r/(1 - T_c)$, where T_c is the firm's marginal tax rate.
 * c. If inflation increases, NPV always falls because the discount rate increases.
   d. Inflation reduces the value of depreciation tax shields.
 * e. If the nominal opportunity cost of capital is 28 percent and expected inflation is 15 percent, the real opportunity cost of capital is 13 percent.

5. Machines A and B cost the same, but have different useful lives and operating costs. Real cash outflows are:

	t=0	t=1	t=2	t=3	t=4	t=5
Machine A	-10	-3	-3	-3	-3 (Replace)	
Machine B	-10	-4	-4	-4	-4	-4 (Replace)

Which of the following statements is/are correct?
   a. B is better because paying out $4 in year 4 is better than paying out $10 to replace A.
 * b. A is better at a discount rate of 10 percent.
 * c. A is better at a discount rate of 20 percent.
   d. B is better at a discount rate of zero.

6. When considering the problem of what to discount, one should always:
   a. Consider only cash flow.
   b. Always make estimates on an incremental basis.
   c. Be consistent in the treatment of inflation.
 * d. All of the above.
   e. None of the above.

7. Which of the following are valid capital budgeting rules?
 * a. Include all incidental effects.
 * b. Include working capital requirements.
   c. Exclude opportunity costs.
   d. Include sunk costs.
   e. All of the above.

8. If the depreciation amount is $100,000 and the marginal tax rate is 35%, then the tax shield due to depreciation is:
   a. $285,714
   b. $100,000
 * c. $ 35,000
   d. None of the above.

9. If the depreciation amount is $200,000 and the marginal tax rate is 40%, then the tax shield due to depreciation is:
 * a. $ 80,000
   b. $200,000
   c. $500,000
   d. None of the above.

10. A project requires an initial investment in equipment of $300,000 and is expected to produce a net cash inflow before taxes of $120,000 per year for three years (i.e., the cash inflows will occur at t=1, t=2, and t=3). The corporate tax rate is 40%. The asset can be depreciated according to the three-year schedule, which allows depreciation of 33.33% at t=1, 44.45% at t=2, 14.81% at t=3, and 7.41% at t=4. At t=3, the company plans to sell the equipment for $30,000. The company's tax situation is such that it can make use of all applicable tax shields. The opportunity cost of capital is 12%. The net present value of this project is:
   a. Less than -$30,000.
 * b. -$17,000
   c. $ 2,000
   d. $15,000
   e. More than $25,000.

11. You own 100 acres of timberland, with young timber worth $20,000 if logged today; this represents 500 cords of wood at $40 per cord. After logging, the land itself could be sold (today) for $10,000 (that is, $100 per acre). The opportunity cost of capital is 10%. You have made the following estimates:
   a. The price of a cord of wood will increase by 5% per year for the foreseeable future.
   b. The price of land will increase by 3% per year for the foreseeable future.
   c. The yearly growth rates of the number of cords of wood on your land are: Years 1-2, 15%; years 3-4, 11%; years 5-8, 5%; year 9 and thereafter, 2%.

The net present value of the optimal decision is:
   a. $30,000
   b. $31,300
   c. $33,700
 * d. $34,700

12. You own 200 acres of timberland, with young timber worth $40,000 if logged today; this represents 1000 cords of wood at $40 per cord. After logging, the land itself could be sold (today) for $30,000 (that is, $150 per acre). The opportunity cost of capital is 6%. You have made the following estimates:
   a. The price of a cord of wood will increase by 4% per year for the foreseeable future.
   b. The price of land will increase by 5% per year for the foreseeable future.
   c. The yearly growth rates of the number of cords of wood on your land are: Years 1-2, 10%; years 3-4, 7%; years 5-8, 4%; year 9 and thereafter, 2%.

The optimal decision is to sell after how many years?
* a. 8 years
  b. 6 years
  c. 4 years
  d. 2 years
  e. None of the above.

13. A project requires an initial investment in equipment of $100,000 and is expected to produce sales revenue of $120,000 the first year (i.e., at t=1); this revenue will increase by 10% per year over the next two years (i.e., t=2 and t=3). Manufacturing costs are estimated to be 70% of sales. The project feasibility study, which was done last year, cost $20,000.
   The asset can be depreciated according to the three-year schedule, which allows depreciation of 33.33% at t=1, 44.45% at t=2, 14.81% at t=3, and 7.41% at t=4. The corporate tax rate is 40%.
   The project requires an investment in working capital. Specifically, at the beginning (i.e., t=0) of the project, $10,000 of working capital is required; thereafter, working capital is projected to be 10% of revenue.
   At t=3, the company plans to sell the equipment for $10,000. The company's tax situation is such that it can make use of all applicable tax shields. To the nearest percent, this project's internal rate of return is:
* a. 7%
  b. 10%
  c. 13%
  d. 17%
  e. 21%

14. A project requires an initial investment of $200,000 and is expected to produce a cash inflow before taxes of $80,000 per year for three years (i.e., the cash inflows will occur at t=1,2, and 3). The corporate tax rate is 34%. The asset can be depreciated according to the three-year schedule, which allows depreciation of 33.33% at t=1, 44.45% at t=2, 14.81% at t=3, and 7.41% at t=4. The company's tax situation is such that it can make use of all applicable tax shields. The opportunity cost of capital is 9%. The project's net present value is:
    a. -$12,500
    b. -$10,700
*   c. -$ 8,800
    d. -$ 5,400
    e. $ 2,200

15. Limey's Products ("Everything For The Modern Classroom") is considering manufacturing a new type of chalk that will never break. The first step is to decide which type of equipment to purchase; each type produces the same amount of chalk, but the costs and lives are different. The equipment types and their associated costs are:

Year	Type A	Type B	Type C
0	$50,000	$60,000	$55,000
1	11,000	9,000	12,000
2	11,000	9,000	12,000
3	11,000 & replace	9,000	12,000 & replace
		9,000 & replace	

Only one type of equipment will be purchased. If the opportunity cost of capital is 15%, what is the Equivalent Annual Cost of the best machine?
    a. $35,100
    b. $32,900
*   c. $30,000
    d. $28,600

16. P&R Products is considering the purchase of a new machine; there are two possibilities, listed below with their associated costs:

Year	Type A	Type B
0	$25,000	$30,000
1	6,000	4,000
2	6,000	4,000
3	6,000 & replace	4,000
		4,000 & replace

Only one type of machine will be purchased. If the opportunity cost of capital is 5%, what is the Equivalent Annual Cost of the best machine?
*   a. $12,460
     b. $13,780
     c. $15,180
     d. $17,290

17. Professional Products is considering the purchase of a new machine; there are two possibilities, listed below with their associated (real) costs:

Year	Type A	Type B
0	$22,000	$30,000
1	5,000	4,000
2	5,000	4,000
3	5,000 & replace	4,000
		4,000 & replace

Only one type of machine will be purchased. The analyst has done the calculations of nominal annuity twice: once at the real rate of 5% and once at a rate of 25% to take into account the effects of inflation. At the rate of 5%, machine ___ appears to be better; at the rate of 25%, machine ___ appears to be better. These blanks should be filled in with:
     a.   A; A
     b.   A; B
*   c.   B; A
     d.   B; B

18. Consider the following project cash flows (stated in thousands of dollars), expressed in real terms:

t=0	t=1	t=2	t=3
-10.00	6.00	8.00	5.00

If the real rate of interest is 4% and the expected rate of inflation is 10%, the cash flows (stated in thousands of dollars), expressed in nominal terms, and the project net present value are:
- a. -10.00, 6.00, 8.00, 5.00; 9.00
- b. -10.00, 6.24, 8.65, 5.62; 9.00
- c. -10.00, 6.60, 9.68, 6.66; 9.00
- d. -10.00, 6.86, 10.47, 7.49; 9.00
- e. -10.00, 6.00, 8.00, 5.00; 7.61
- f. -10.00, 6.24, 8.65, 5.62; 7.61
- * g. -10.00, 6.60, 9.68, 6.66; 7.61
- h. -10.00, 6.86, 10.47, 7.49; 7.61

19. Your company is considering buying a machine with the following real costs:

Year	Cost
0	$10,000
1	3,000
2	3,000
3	3,000 & replace

The real rate of interest is 4%. Suppose that technological change is expected to reduce costs by 5% per year; that is, there will be machines in year 1 that cost 5% less to buy and operate than this machine, and similarly in year 2, etc. What is the equivalent annual cost of the machine under consideration?
- a. $3,000
- b. $6,603
- c. $6,453
- d. $6,909
- * e. $6,317

20. Your company is considering buying a machine with the following real costs:

Year	Cost
0	$20,000
1	5,000
2	5,000
3	5,000 & replace

The real rate of interest is 7%. Suppose that technological change is expected to reduce costs by 7% per year; that is, there will be machines in year 1 that cost 7% less to buy and operate than this machine, and similarly in year 2, etc. What is the equivalent annual cost of the machine under consideration?

    a. $ 5,000
    b. $12,621
    c. $ 8,750
*   d. $11,967
    e. $11,667

Chapter 6 - True-False Questions

F   1. When calculating cash flows, make sure that you deduct a realistic forecast of depreciation. Do not accept the accountant's figure for depreciation at face value.

T   2. It is important to consider all incidental effects, such as the effect of a railroad branch line on the traffic it brings to the main line.

T   3. Sunk costs are unaffected by the decision to accept or reject a project and should therefore be ignored.

F   4. The investment decision should be based on average rather than incremental payoffs.

T   5. If an investment project would make use of land which the firm currently owns, the project should be charged with the opportunity cost of that land.

F   6. In capital budgeting, it is important always to deduct the project's share of overhead costs.

F   7. By undertaking the analysis of capital expenditures in real terms, the financial manager avoids having to forecast inflation.

T   8. (1 + real interest rate) = (1 + nominal interest rate) divided by (1 + inflation rate).

F   9. It does not matter whether you discount real cash flows at the nominal interest rate or nominal cash flows at the real rate. The important thing is to be consistent.

F   10. Do not forget to deduct interest and dividend payments when calculating the project's cash flows.

T   11. An investment should be postponed as long as the opportunity cost of capital is less than the rate at which the project's value is growing.

T   12. The rule for comparing machines with different lives is to select the machine with the lowest equivalent annual cost. This is the net present value of the cost of the machine divided by the annuity factor.

T   13. You can think of a machine's equivalent annual cost as the fair rental charge for the machine's services.

T   14.   You should replace a machine when the equivalent annual cost of continuing to operate it exceeds the equivalent annual cost of a new machine.

F   15.   When a resource is freely traded in a market, its opportunity cost is difficult to measure.

F   16.   The most important components of working capital are inventory, accounts payable, and cash.

T   17.   Depreciation is a non-cash expense; it is important only because it reduces taxable income.

F   18.   Depreciation provides an annual tax shield equal to the sum of the depreciation amount and the marginal tax rate.

F   19.   Compared to straight line depreciation, accelerated depreciation provides a smaller tax shield.

T   20.   Almost every large corporation keeps two sets of books, one for its stockholders and one for the Internal Revenue Service.

F   21.   Every project with a positive net present value should be undertaken immediately if at all possible.

Chapter 6 - Essay Questions

1. Discuss why it is important to estimate cash flows on an incremental basis. What are some of the specific cash flows that must be considered?

Answer

The value of a project depends on the cash flows generated by the project; that is, we must analyze the difference in company cash flow between "the company without the project" and "the company with the project." These are the incremental cash flows: any cash flow which changes because the company accepted the project. These include, for example, changes in net working capital (i.e., inventory, receivables, and payables) and opportunity costs associated with the use of resources already owned by the company. These probably exclude allocated overhead costs, but these must be carefully evaluated on a case-by-case basis.

2. Discuss the importance of inflation in the capital budgeting decision. How should inflation be taken into consideration?

Answer

Inflation is a critical concern in capital budgeting because it affects the magnitude of future cash flows as well as the magnitude of nominal interest rates. The key is to treat inflation consistently: Either use estimates of real cash flows in conjunction with a real interest rate, or use estimates of nominal cash flows in conjunction with a nominal interest rate.

Chapter 7 - Multiple Choice Questions

1. What has been the average annual real rate of interest on Treasury bills over the past sixty-nine years?
   * a. Less than 1 percent.
   b. Between 1 and 2 percent.
   c. Between 2 and 8 percent.
   d. More than 8 percent.

2. What has been the average risk premium on common stocks over the past sixty-nine years?
   a. Less than 3 percent.
   b. Between 3 and 6 percent.
   * c. Between 6 and 10 percent.
   d. More than 10 percent.

3. What has been the annual standard deviation of return of the stock market over the past sixty-nine years?
   a. Less than 5 percent.
   b. Between 5 and 10 percent.
   c. Between 10 and 15 percent.
   * d. More than 15 percent.

4. Which portfolio has had the highest average annual real return over the past sixty-nine years?
   a. Treasury bills.
   b. Government bonds.
   c. Corporate bonds.
   d. Common stocks.
   * e. Small-firm common stocks.

5. Which portfolio has had the highest average annual nominal return over the past sixty-nine years?
   a. Treasury bills.
   b. Government bonds.
   c. Corporate bonds.
   d. Common stocks.
   * e. Small-firm common stocks.

6. Which portfolio has had the highest average risk premium over the past sixty-nine years?
   * a. Small-firm common stocks.
   b. Common stocks.
   c. Corporate bonds.
   d. Government bonds.
   e. Treasury bills.

7. Which portfolio has had the highest standard deviation of return over the past sixty-nine years?
   * a. Small-firm common stocks.
   b. Common stocks.
   c. Corporate bonds.
   d. Government bonds.
   e. Treasury bills.

8. What is the standard deviation of a well-diversified portfolio of stocks with an average beta of 1.21?
   a. 1.1 times the standard deviation of r_m.
   * b. 1.21 times the standard deviation of r_m.
   c. The same as the standard deviation of r_m.
   d. Can't say without knowing the correlations between the stocks.

9. What is the standard deviation of a poorly diversified portfolio of stocks with an average beta of .8?
   a. Less than .8 times the standard deviation of r_m.
   * b. More than .8 times the standard deviation of r_m.
   c. The same as the standard deviation of r_m.
   d. Can't say.

10. Sam Spinach has divided his money evenly between General Mills and Bristol Myers. On past evidence both stocks have a standard deviation of 20 percent. Suppose the correlation between General Mills and Bristol Myers were +1.0. What is the standard deviation of Mr. Spinach's portfolio?
    a. Less than 20 percent because the portfolio is diversified.
    * b. Exactly 20 percent.
    c. More than 20 percent because of the unique risk.
    d. Need more information to solve.

11. Tracy Turnip has invested two-thirds of her money in General Mills stock and the remainder in Holly Sugar. On past evidence, the standard deviation is 20 percent for General Mills and 40 percent for Holly Sugar. Suppose the correlation between General Mills and Holly Sugar were -1.0. What is the standard deviation of Ms. Turnip's portfolio?
    * a. 0 percent.
    b. 15.2 percent.
    c. 26.6 percent.
    d. 30.0 percent.

12. Suppose that the average standard deviation of return on each individual stock is 40 percent per year and that the average correlation between each pair of stocks is .25. What is the annual standard deviation of return of a well-diversified portfolio?
    a. 40 percent.
    b. 10 percent.
*   c. 20 percent.
    d. Can't say without knowing the stocks' betas.

13. If stock A has a 40% chance of gaining 20% and a 60% chance of losing 10%, the expected return of stock A is:
    a. 20%
    b. -10%
*   c. 2%
    d. 5%

14. If stock A has a 40% chance of gaining 20% and a 60% chance of losing 10%, the standard deviation of return of stock A is:
    a. 0%
    b. 37%
    c. 30%
*   d. 15%

15. If stock B has a 70% chance of gaining 40% and a 30% chance of losing 20%, the expected return of stock B is:
    a. 13%
    b. 34%
    c. 28%
*   d. 22%

16. If stock B has a 70% chance of gaining 40% and a 30% chance of losing 20%, the standard deviation of return of stock B is:
    a. 0%
*   b. 27%
    c. 31%
    d. 35%

17. If a stock has a covariance with the market portfolio of .032 and if the standard deviation of the market portfolio's return is .20, the stock has a beta of:
    a. 6.25
    b. .03
    c. .16
*   d. .80
    e. None of the above.

18. If a stock has a covariance with the market portfolio of .060 and if the standard deviation of the market portfolio's return is .20, the stock has a beta of:
    a.   .02
    b.   1.20
    c.   .09
    d.   .30
*   e.   None of the above.

19. The standard deviation of the market portfolio return has been highest in which time period?
    a.   1980-1994
    b.   1970-1979
    c.   1960-1969
    d.   1950-1959
    e.   1940-1949
*   f.   1926-1939

20. Consider two long-lived projects, A and B, with present values as follows:
$$PV_A = 350 \quad \text{at} \quad r = .12$$
$$PV_B = 400 \quad \text{at} \quad r = .18$$

Suppose the two assets are combined into a composite asset AB; the cash flows of AB equal the sums of the cash flows of A and B separately. Then the present value of AB:
    a.   Must be calculated by discounting AB's cash flows at (12 + 18) / 2 = 15 percent.
*   b.   Equals 350 + 400, or 750.
    c.   Can't answer without knowing the standard deviations of A and B.
    d.   Can't answer without knowing the betas of A and B.

Chapter 7 - True-False Questions

T   1. Annual rates of return from common stocks fluctuate so much that it is necessary to take a very long time period to estimate their average rate of return.

T   2. If we are evaluating a project of average risk, we can discount the cash flows at the expected return on the average common stock, which historical evidence suggests is 8 to 9 percent above the risk-free rate.

F   3. The standard statistical measures of spread are variance and standard deviation, which is simply the square of the variance.

F   4. The variability of a portfolio's rate of return is only slightly larger than that of individual securities.

T   5. Diversification reduces risk because prices of different stocks do not move exactly together.

F   6. The risk that potentially can be eliminated by diversification is called market risk.

T   7. The risk that potentially can be eliminated by diversification is called unique risk.

T   8. The risk that cannot be eliminated by diversification is called market risk.

F   9. The risk that cannot be eliminated by diversification is called unique risk.

T   10. The risk of a well-diversified portfolio depends on the market risk of the securities included in the portfolio.

T   11. The sensitivity of an investment's return to market movements is usually called its beta.

F   12. The average beta of all stocks is zero.

T   13. A well-diversified portfolio of stocks with an average beta of 2.0 is twice as variable as the market portfolio.

F   14. Stocks with a beta of zero offer an expected return of zero.

F   15. Beta is defined as $(\sigma_i \sigma_m / \sigma_m^2)$.

T   16. The ratio (σ_{im}/σ_m^2) measures a stock's contribution to portfolio risk.

T   17.   If investors can diversify on their own account, they will not pay any extra for firms that diversify.

T   18.   The expected return on a portfolio is a weighted average of the expected returns on the individual securities.

F   19.   The standard deviation of returns on a portfolio is equal to the weighted average of the standard deviations of the returns on the individual securities if these returns are completely uncorrelated.

F   20.   Because investors cannot hope to make large speculative profits from investing in Treasury bills, the expected return from bills has to be higher than the expected return from the market portfolio.

Chapter 7 - Essay Questions

1. Discuss the importance of beta as a risk measure for a single security.

Answer
      Any single security has both unique risk and market risk; it is the market risk that is measured by beta. If the stock is held by itself, then indeed beta is unimportant: What is critical is the total risk, that is, the sum of the market risk and the unique risk. However, because of the benefits of diversification, investors will not just hold one security, but instead will hold a portfolio of securities. In this case, the unique risk of each security is diversified away, and it is the market risk (beta) which is left. Thus, in the context of a well-diversified portfolio, beta measures a single security's contribution to the portfolio's risk.

2. Suppose you are relatively young and are contemplating an investment strategy for your personal pension fund. What investments would you consider and why?

Answer
      Considering the five general types of investments - Treasury bills, government bonds, corporate bonds, common stocks, small-firm common stocks - there are clear differences in risk and expected return, as reflected in the historical averages. However, for someone investing for the long term, and who would therefore not be concerned about year-to-year fluctuations, the small-firm common stocks would be preferred because they have yielded the highest average return.

Chapter 8 - Multiple Choice Questions

1. Portfolio A has an expected return of 10 percent and a standard deviation of 21 percent. Portfolio B has an expected return of 15 percent and a standard deviation of 24 percent. If these are the only investments available, what should an investor do?
    a. Invest entirely in A.
    b. Invest entirely in B.
    c. Invest half in A and half in B.
*   d. Can't say without knowing the investor's degree of risk aversion.

2. Portfolio C has an expected return of 12 percent and a standard deviation of 18 percent. Portfolio D has an expected return of 14 percent and a standard deviation of 20 percent. If investors can borrow and lend at an interest rate of 8 percent, they should:
    a. Prefer portfolio C to portfolio D.
*   b. Prefer portfolio D to portfolio C.
    c. Be indifferent between portfolios C and D.
    d. Can't say without knowing investor's degree of risk aversion.

3. Efficient portfolios are those which offer:
*   a. The highest expected return for a given level of risk.
    b. The highest risk for a given level of expected return.
    c. The minimum level of risk and expected return.
    d. The maximum level of risk and expected return.

4. According to the capital asset pricing model, all investments must:
    a. Offer the same level of expected return.
    b. Lie along the same line as efficient portfolios.
    c. Offer the same level of market risk.
*   d. Lie along the security market line.

5. If investors can borrow and lend at the risk-free rate of interest, then they should:
    a. Always invest in the market portfolio.
    b. Always invest in the risk-free investment.
*   c. Always hold a mixture of the risk-free investment and the market portfolio.
    d. Always invest in the portfolio with the minimum level of risk.

6. Bernard Bontebok borrows $10,000 at 8 percent and invests this together with $5,000 of his own money in a portfolio of common stocks. If the stock portfolio has a standard deviation of 24 percent, what is the standard deviation of the return to Mr. Bontebok's $5,000 equity investment?
    a. 24 percent.
    b. 48 percent.
*   c. 72 percent.
    d. None of the above.

7. Which of these strategies should offer Jack the same expected return as a stock with a beta of 1.5?
    a. Investing a third of his money in Treasury bills and investing the remainder in the market portfolio.
    b. Borrowing an amount equal to one-third of his own resources and investing everything in the market portfolio.
*   c. Borrowing an amount equal to one-half of his own resources and investing everything in the market portfolio.
    d. None of the above.

8. According to the capital asset pricing model, the only reason expected returns differ is:
    a. Variance.
*   b. Beta.
    c. The market portfolio.
    d. The risk-free investment.

9. Empirical rests have shown that the capital asset pricing model:
*   a. Holds up pretty well over long time periods but not over short time periods.
    b. Holds up pretty well over short time periods but not over long time periods.
    c. Incorporates risks not captured by beta.
    d. Is useless and should be replaced by the arbitrage pricing theory.

10. In theory, the capital asset pricing model requires that the market portfolio include:
    a. Common stocks.
    b. Bonds.
    c. Real estate.
    d. Human capital.
*   e. All of the above.

11. The expected return on the market portfolio is 20%, and the risk-free rate of return is 8%. An investment has a beta of 1.4 and offers an expected return of 23%.
    a. This is a good investment because it earns more than the market rate of return.
*   b. This investment has a negative net present value.
    c. This investment has a positive net present value.
    d. Need more information to decide if this is a good or bad investment.

12. The expected return on the market portfolio is 15%, and the risk-free rate of return is 5%. An investment has a beta of .8 and offers an expected return of 15%.
    a. This is a good investment because it earns more than the market rate of return.
    b. This investment has a negative net present value.
*   c. This investment has a positive net present value.
    d. Need more information to decide if this is a good or bad investment.

13. The expected return on the market portfolio is 12%, and the risk-free rate of return is 4%. An investment has a beta of .6 and offers an expected return of 8%.
    a. This is a good investment because it earns more than the market rate of return.
*   b. This investment has a negative net present value.
    c. This investment has a positive net present value.
    d. Need more information to decide if this is a good or bad investment.

14. The expected return on the market portfolio is 17%, and the risk-free rate of return is 9%. An investment has a beta of 1.8 and offers an expected return of 26%.
    a. This is a good investment because it earns more than the market rate of return.
    b. This investment has a negative net present value.
*   c. This investment has a positive net present value.
    d. Need more information to decide if this is a good or bad investment.

15. A company is deciding whether to issue stock to raise money for an investment project which has the same risk as the market and an expected return of 15%. If the risk-free rate is 5% and the expected return on the market is 12%, the company should go ahead:
    a. This is false: The company should not take this project.
*   b. Whatever the company's beta.
    c. Unless the company's beta is greater than 1.25.
    d. Unless the company's beta is less than 1.25.

16. A company is deciding whether to issue stock to raise money for an investment project which has the same risk as the market and an expected return of 15%. If the risk-free rate is 5% and the expected return on the market is 12%, the company should go ahead:
*   a. Whatever the company's beta.
    b. Unless the company's beta is greater than 1.25.
    c. Unless the company's beta is less than 1.25.
    d. Need more information to solve.

17. The stock of Charles & Co. has a beta of 1.0 and a very high unique risk. If the expected return on the market is 15%, the expected return on Charles & Co. will be:
*   a. 15%
    b. Less than 15%.
    c. More than 15%.
    d. Must know the risk-free rate to solve.

18. The stock of Roger's has a beta of 1.0 and a very high unique risk. If the expected return on the market is 12%, the expected return on Roger's will be:
    a. Must know the risk-free rate to solve.
    b. Less than 12%.
    c. More than 12%.
*   d. 12%.

19. Arbitrage pricing theory implies that there are higher risk premiums on stocks with returns that are especially sensitive to:
    a. Changes in long-term interest rates.
    b. Changes in short-term interest rates.
    c. The market portfolio.
    d. Oil price changes.
*   e. None of the above.

20. The arbitrage pricing theory implies that there are higher risk premiums on stocks with returns that are especially sensitive to:
    a. The yield spread.
    b. Interest rates.
    c. Exchange rates.
    d. Real GNP.
*   e. None of the above.

21. The arbitrage pricing theory states that:
    a. All stocks with the same beta have the same expected return, because otherwise investors could arbitrage within a beta "class."
    b. The expected return on a portfolio with returns uncorrelated with any of the model's underlying factors will equal zero.
    c. There are two factors that will be important in security pricing: an interest rate factor and a business cycle factor, the latter usually measured by changes in industrial production.
*   d. Any stock's expected risk premium is a weighted average of expected risk premiums on the underlying factors.

Chapter 8 - True-False Questions

F   1. If two investment strategies offer the same expected return, most investors would prefer the one with the higher variance.

F   2. If stock A has an expected return of 12% and a standard deviation of return of 10%, and stock B has an expected return of 14% and a standard deviation of return of 8%, then most investors would prefer stock A.

T   3. Portfolios that offer the highest expected return for a given variance or standard deviation are known as efficient portfolios.

T   4. The investor's job can be divided into two stages. The first is to select the "best" portfolio of common stocks; the second is to blend this portfolio with borrowing or lending to obtain an exposure to risk that suits his/her particular tastes.

T   5. If an investor has the same information as everybody else, his/her best stock portfolio is the same as for everybody else, i.e., the market portfolio.

F   6. In a competitive market, the expected risk premium varies inversely with beta.

T.   7. According to the capital asset pricing model, all investments plot along the security market line.

F   8. A stock's sensitivity to changes in the value of the market portfolio is measured by that stock's variance of return.

T   9. Beta measures the marginal contribution of a stock to the risk of a portfolio.

F   10. You can construct a portfolio with a beta of .75 by investing three-quarters of your money in Treasury bills and the remainder in the market portfolio.

T   11. If a portfolio is efficient, there must be a straight line relationship between each stock's expected return and its marginal contribution to portfolio risk.

F   12. Investors are principally concerned with those risks that can be eliminated through diversification.

T   13. The capital asset pricing model is equivalent to the statement that the market portfolio is efficient.

F   14.   From the early 1960s through 1990, small-company stocks performed substantially worse than large-company stocks.

T   15.   Tests of the capital asset pricing model are made more difficult by the fact that one cannot observe expected returns.

F   16.   In theory, the capital asset pricing model requires that the market portfolio consist of all common stocks.

T   17.   In the consumption capital asset pricing model, uncertainty about stock returns is connected directly to uncertainty about consumption.

F   18.   The arbitrage pricing theory implies that the market portfolio is efficient.

T   19.   The difference between the capital asset pricing model and the arbitrage pricing theory is that the former assumes that only one type of risk (the sensitivity to the market factor) earns a risk premium.

F   20.   The arbitrage pricing theory states that each stock's risk premium depends on two things: the risk premium associated with each factor and the stock's sensitivity to the market.

T   21.   Both the capital asset pricing model and the arbitrage pricing theory stress that expected return is not affected by unique risk.

F   22.   The arbitrage pricing theory specifies the key macroeconomic factors underlying stock returns.

Chapter 8 - Essay Questions

1. Compare the capital asset pricing model and the arbitrage pricing model, noting carefully their similarities and differences.

Answer

The capital asset pricing model (CAPM) and the arbitrage pricing theory (APT) are similar in that both state expected returns depend on risk stemming from economy-wide influences; that is, unique risk does not affect expected return.

The CAPM, however, is based on a set of very restrictive assumptions that, for example, investors only care about expected return and variance of return, all investors can borrow or lend at the risk-free rate of return, etc. Because of these restrictive assumptions, the CAPM only has one "risk factor," the market portfolio, thus making it relatively easy to use in practice.

The APT has no restrictive assumptions, which is a plus; the problem is that the APT does not specify which macroeconomic factors are the important ones, which makes it difficult to use the APT in practice.

2. Discuss how you would use the arbitrage pricing theory to estimate the cost of equity for a company.

Answer

There are several necessary steps here:

1. Identify the macroeconomic factors. The key problem here, of course, is that there is no theory to guide the choice of factors, nor even to guide the number of factors chosen. Elton, Gruber, and Mei (see text) used six: yield spread, interest rate, exchange rate, real GNP, inflation, and the portion of the market return not explained by the first five.

2. Estimate the risk premium for each factor. This is a critical step because different stocks will be exposed to different factors to differing degrees.

3. Estimate the factor sensitivities. Here we estimate the sensitivity of a particular company's common stock to the different factors.

Because the arbitrage pricing theory states that the risk premium for any asset depends upon its sensitivities to factor risks and the expected risk premium for each factor, the end result is the company's stock's expected return.

Chapter 9 - Multiple Choice Questions

1. The true cost of capital for a project depends on:
   * a. The use to which the capital is put, i.e., the project.
   b. The company's cost of capital.
   c. The industry-wide cost of capital.
   d. All of the above.

2. If a company uses the same company cost of capital for evaluating all projects, which of the following results is likely?
   a. Accepting poor low-risk projects.
   b. Rejecting good high-risk projects.
   c. Both a and b.
   * d. Neither a nor b.

3. If a company uses the same company cost of capital for evaluating all projects, which of the following results is likely?
   a. Rejecting good low-risk projects.
   b. Accepting poor high-risk projects.
   * c. Both a and b.
   d. Neither a nor b.

4. Using the company cost of capital to evaluate a project is:
   a. Always incorrect.
   b. Always correct.
   c. Correct only for those companies which have a low standard error of beta.
   * d. Correct for projects that are about as risky as the average of the company's other assets.

5. In a graph with "change in price of common stock" on the vertical (Y) axis and "change in market index" on the horizontal (X) axis, the slope of the regression line represents the stock's:
   a. Alpha.
   * b. Beta.
   c. R-squared.
   d. Adjusted beta.

6. If a company changes its financial structure:
   a. Its debt beta will not change.
   b. Its common stock beta will not change.
   * c. Its asset beta will not change.
   d. All of the above.

7. The market value of Charon Ferries' common stock is $16 million, and the market value of its (risk-free) debt is $4 million. The beta of the company's common stock is 1.5, and the expected risk premium on the market is 8 percent. If the Treasury bill rate is 5 percent, what is the company's cost of capital?
  a. 13.0 percent.
* b. 14.6 percent.
  c. 17.0 percent.
  d. 20.0 percent.

8. The market value of Ralph's Inc. common stock is $20 million, and the market value of its (risk-free) debt is $5 million. The beta of the company's common stock is 1.2, and the expected risk premium on the market is 7 percent. If the Treasury bill rate is 3 percent, what is the company's cost of capital?
* a. 9.7 percent.
  b. 10.0 percent.
  c. 11.4 percent.
  d. 15.6 percent.

9. The market value of XYZ Corp. common stock is $6 million, and the market value of its (risk-free) debt is $4 million. The beta of the company's common stock is 2.3, and the expected risk premium on the market is 8 percent. If the Treasury bill rate is 4 percent, what is the company's cost of capital?
  a. 12.0 percent.
* b. 15.0 percent.
  c. 11.4 percent.
  d. 22.4 percent.

10. Sweeny Pie Company's common stock has a beta of 1.0 and a total market value of $12 million. The expected risk premium on the market is 8 percent, and the Treasury bill rate is 12 percent. If the company's cost of capital is 18 percent, what is the value of the company's (risk-free) debt?
  a. 0
  b. $2 million.
* c. $4 million.
  d. $8 million.

11. Myers & Co. has a company cost of capital of 20.0%. The company is financed with $15 million of (risk-free) debt and $10 million of common stock, which has a beta of 1.8. The risk-free rate is 5%, and the expected return on the market portfolio is 15%. If the company issues $10 million more common stock, the new company cost of capital will be:
*   a.   20.0%
     b.   15.3%
     c.   23.0%
     d.   Need more information to solve.

12. Meredith Corp. is financed with $25 million of (risk-free) debt and $50 million of common stock, which has a beta of 1.6. The risk-free rate is 4%, and the expected return on the market portfolio is 13%. If the company issues $25 million more common stock and uses the proceeds to buy back all the outstanding debt, the company cost of capital will be:
     a.   4.0%
     b.   18.4%
     c.   17.0%
*   d.   13.6%

13. Meredith Corp. is financed with $25 million of (risk-free) debt and $50 million of common stock, which has a beta of 1.6. The risk-free rate is 4%, and the expected return on the market portfolio is 13%. If the company issues $25 million more common stock and uses the proceeds to buy back all the outstanding debt, the cost of equity capital will be:
     a.   4.0%
     b.   18.4%
     c.   17.0%
*   d.   13.6%

14. Consider the following market-value balance sheet:

Assets	200	50	Debt (D)
	___	150	Equity (E)
	200	200	Market value (V)

β_{equity} = .8 and the debt is risk free. Now suppose this firm announces an issue of $120 of additional debt. All the proceeds of the debt issue are paid out as a special dividend. After these changes, the market value of old debt falls to $40 and β_{debt} is .3. What is the new β_{equity}?
     a.   .9
     b.   1.5
*   c.   1.8
     d.   2.0
     e.   3.0

15. Which of the following characteristics are likely to be associated with a high company cost of capital?
    a. High operating leverage.
    b. High fixed costs.
    c. Cyclical revenues.
*   d. All of the above.

16. Estimated project cash flows should:
*   a. Represent a probability-weighted average of future cash flows.
    b. Reflect the most likely outcomes.
    c. Incorporate conservative assumptions about revenues, operating costs, etc.; the degree of conservatism should increase with project beta.
    d. Represent cash flows that will be received if the firm meets its budgeted targets for revenues, operating costs, etc.; the risks of not meeting targets are offset by using a higher hurdle rate.

17. A project has an expected cash flow of $200 in each of years 1 and 2. $r_f = .10$, $r_m = .18$, and the project's $\beta = 1.5$. If it is appropriate to use a constant risk-adjusted discount rate, what is the certainty-equivalent cash flow in year 2?
    a. $134
*   b. $163
    c. $175
    d. $200

18. A project has an expected cash flow of $500 in each of years 1 and 2. $r_f = .05$, $r_m = .15$, and the project's $\beta = 0.8$. If it is appropriate to use a constant risk-adjusted discount rate, what is the certainty-equivalent cash flow in year 2?
*   a. $432
    b. $400
    c. $417
    d. $500

19. A project has an expected cash flow of $300 in each of years one through five. $r_f = .04$, $r_m = .12$, and the project's $\beta = 1.7$. If it is appropriate to use a constant risk-adjusted discount rate, what is the certainty-equivalent cash flow in year 3?
    a. $510
*   b. $235
    c. $259
    d. $300

20. What does use of a constant risk-adjusted discount rate imply about the certainty equivalents of project cash flows? Assume expected project cash flows are constant over time.
    a.   CEQs are constant over time.
    b.   CEQs decline linearly; e.g., $CEQ_1 = .90$, $CEQ_2 = .80$, $CEQ_3 = .70$, etc.
*   c.   CEQs decline geometrically; e.g., $CEQ_1 = .90$, $CEQ_2 = .81$, $CEQ_3 = .73$, etc.
    d.   CEQs increase at a rate which depends on project beta.

Chapter 9 - True-False Questions

T   1. The expected rate of return on a portfolio of all the firm's securities is known as the "company cost of capital."

F   2. The company cost of capital is the correct discount rate for any project undertaken by that company.

T   3. Each project should be evaluated at its own opportunity cost of capital; the true cost of capital depends on the use to which the capital is put.

F   4. The capital asset pricing theory tells us to accept any project offering a return that more than compensates for the company's beta.

T   5. To estimate common stock betas from historical data, you can plot past returns on the stock (vertical axis) against past returns on the market (horizontal axis). The estimated beta is the slope of the line fitted through these points.

F   6. If companies' risk characteristics did not change, it would be possible to obtain perfectly accurate estimates of beta from, say, five years of historical data.

T   7. It's generally more accurate to estimate an "industry beta" for a portfolio of companies in the same industry than to estimate beta for a single company.

F   8. Financial leverage affects the risk (and hence the expected return) of the firm's assets.

T   9. Financial leverage affects the risk (and hence the expected return) of the firm's common stock.

F   10. The beta of a portfolio of all the firm's securities is generally more than the beta of its common stock.

T   11. The beta of a portfolio of all the firm's securities is a weighted average of the betas on the individual securities.

F   12. If a company is financed equally by common stock and (risk-free) debt and if the beta of the common stock is 1.0, then the beta of the firm's assets is 2.0.

T   13. Estimates of the company cost of capital should be based on the beta of the firm's assets.

F   14. Companies with cyclical revenues tend to have lower asset betas.

T   15.   Companies with high operating leverage tend to have higher asset betas.

F   16.   The difference between a company's equity beta and its asset betas reflects business risk.

T   17.   Project NPVs should be calculated using probability-weighted averages of future cash flows.

F   18.   When calculating project NPVs, always discount the most likely future cash flows at the project's opportunity cost of capital.

T   19.   Risky projects can be evaluated by discounting the expected cash flows at a risk-adjusted discount rate or by discounting certainty equivalent cash flows at the risk-free interest rate.

F   20.   Using the same risk-adjusted discount rate to discount all cash flows ignores the fact that the more distant cash flows are more risky.

T   21.   Using the same risk-adjusted discount rate to discount all cash flows assumes that risk increases at a constant rate as you look farther out into the future.

Chapter 9 - Essay Questions

1. Discuss how you would estimate the cost of capital for a project that was about as risky as the other assets of the firm.

Answer

If a project is approximately as risky as the other assets of the firm, the appropriate discount rate is the company cost of capital. One way to estimate this is to estimate the required rate of return on each of the company's securities (debt, preferred stock, and common stock) and then use the weighted average of these, where the weights are the proportions of the firm financed by each type of security.

2. Discuss why one might use an industry beta to estimate a company's cost of capital.

Answer

Any single estimate of beta is usually relatively imprecise, that is, has a large standard error. If a company is similar to others within a particular industry - where 'similar' is admittedly difficult to define - then the industry beta can be used as an estimate of the company's beta. The advantage of such a procedure is that an industry beta can be estimated much more precisely than the beta of any single company within that industry. One, of course, must make the necessary adjustments for differing capital structures.

3. Discuss the relationship between the risk-adjusted approach to estimating present value and the certainty equivalent approach.

Answer

The risk-adjusted approach uses one number, the discount rate, to adjust for both risk and the time value of money. The advantage is simplicity; the difficulty is that the project's risk may not be well behaved.

The certainty equivalent approach allows for much more generality; the individual factors (the a_ts) can be allowed to vary in any desired pattern to account for the risk of the cash flows, while the risk-free rate is used to adjust for the time value of money. This flexibility has a price, however: Someone has to specify all these parameters.

If the cash flows of the project have the same market risk at each point in time, these approaches are equivalent.

Chapter 10 - Multiple Choice Questions

1. The benefits of sensitivity analysis include:
    a. It provides estimates of the expected, optimistic, and pessimistic values for total project cash flows.
*   b. It forces the manager to identify the key underlying variables, indicates where additional information would be most useful, and helps to expose confused forecasts.
    c. It helps the manager to judge whether the return is adequate compensation for the risks involved.
    d. All of the above.

2. You have come up with the following estimates of project cash flows:

	Pessimistic Estimate	Expectation	Optimistic Estimate
Investment	-160	-100	-60
Annual Sales	+15	+20	+25
Annual Costs	-12	-10	-6

The cash flows are perpetual and the cost of capital is 10 percent. What does a sensitivity analysis of NPV with respect to annual costs show?

	Pessimistic Estimate	Expectation	Optimistic Estimate
a.	-130	0	+310
b.	-20	0	+130
c.	-130	0	+40
* d.	-130	0	+130

3. You have come up with the following estimates of project cash flows:

	Pessimistic Estimate	Expectation	Optimistic Estimate
Investment	-200	-100	-50
Annual Sales	+30	+50	+80
Annual Costs	-25	-20	-15

The cash flows are perpetual and the cost of capital is 10 percent. What does a sensitivity analysis of NPV with respect to annual costs show?

	Pessimistic Estimate	Expectation	Optimistic Estimate
* a.	-150	+200	+600
b.	-50	+200	+600
c.	-150	+200	+650
d.	-195	-70	+15

4. You have come up with the following estimates of project cash flows:

	Pessimistic Estimate	Expectation	Optimistic Estimate
Investment	-100	-80	-60
Annual Sales	+30	+40	+50
Annual Costs	-20	-15	-10

The cash flows are perpetual and the cost of capital is 5 percent. What does a sensitivity analysis of NPV with respect to annual costs show?

	Pessimistic Estimate	Expectation	Optimistic Estimate
a.	+200	+420	+800
b.	0	+500	-10
* c.	+100	+420	+740
d.	-90	-55	-20

5. United Boot proposes to invest $5 million in new boot-making equipment. Fixed costs are $1 million a year. A pair of boots costs $5 to manufacture and can be sold for $10. If the equipment lasts for 10 years and the cost of capital is 8 percent, what is the break-even level of annual sales?
    a. 211,463 pairs.
    b. 300,426 pairs.
*   c. 349,029 pairs
    d. 363,124 pairs.

6. Often firms calculate a project's break-even sales using book earnings. Break-even sales based on book earnings are generally ___?___ sales based on project NPV.
    a. Higher than.
*   b. Lower than.
    c. The same as.
    d. Can't say without knowing project life.

7. John Shoe, Inc. proposes to invest $3 million in new knife-making equipment. Fixed costs are $.5 million a year. A knife costs $7 to manufacture and can be sold for $14. If the equipment lasts for 8 years and the cost of capital is 12 percent, what is the break-even level of annual sales?
*   a. 157,695 knives.
    b. 586,266 knives.
    c. 86,266 knives.
    d. 603,865 knives.

8. Post, Inc. proposes to invest $4 million in new tool-making equipment. Fixed costs are $2 million a year. A tool costs $10 to manufacture and can be sold for $12. If the equipment lasts for 20 years and the cost of capital is 6 percent, what is the break-even level of annual sales?
    a.   348,736 tools.
    b.   174,368 tools.
    c.   2,174,368 tools.
*   d.   1,174,368 tools.

9. Which of the following statements *does not* apply to simulation models of investment projects?
    a.   They enable the financial manager to analyze what would happen if the uncertainty about any of the variables were reduced.
    b.   They take into account the interdependencies between different time periods.
*   c.   They are easily communicated and understood.
    d.   They enable the financial manager to see how outcomes may be affected if the project is modified.

10. Which of the following statements *does not* apply to simulation models of investment projects?
*   a.   They enable the financial manager to appraise risky projects without estimating the opportunity cost of capital.
    b.   They usually ignore opportunities to expand or abandon the project.
    c.   They are complex and expensive to develop.
    d.   They are specific to the project being analyzed; that is, every project requires a new simulation model.

11. Which of the following simulation outputs is likely to be most useful and easy to interpret? The output shows the distribution(s) of the project's:
    a.   Earnings.
    b.   Internal rate of return.
    c.   NPV calculated using the opportunity cost of capital.
    d.   NPV calculated using the risk-free interest rate.
*   e.   Cash flows.

12. Simulation models are useful:
    a.   To understand the project better.
    b.   To forecast expected cash flows.
    c.   To assess project risk.
*   d.   All of the above.

13. Which of the following statements applies to decision trees?
* a. They require the financial manager to identify the principal things that could happen to the project and the main actions that the company might take.
   b. They should include all possible future events and decisions.
   c. They eliminate the need to calculate the opportunity cost of capital.
   d. All of the above.

14. Which of the following statements applies to decision trees?
   a. They are simply to construct and analyze.
   b. They should include all possible future events and decisions.
* c. They help the manager to assess the value of options to abandon or expand the project.
   d. All of the above.

15. Monte Carlo simulation is likely to be the most useful:
   a. If a small amount of money is at stake.
* b. If a large amount of money is at stake.
   c. If a moderate amount of money is at stake.
   d. Regardless of the amount of money at stake.

16. Monte Carlo simulation is likely to be the most useful:
   a. For simple problems.
   b. For problems of moderate complexity.
* c. For very complex problems.
   d. Regardless of the problem's complexity.

17. Monte Carlo simulation is likely to be the most useful:
   a. In large companies that require major investments.
* b. In large companies that make many small investments.
   c. In small companies that make many small investments.
   d. All of the above.

18. Monte Carlo simulation is likely to be the most useful:
* a. In the pharmaceutical industry.
   b. In the food processing industry.
   c. In the retail shoe industry.
   d. None of the above.

19. Given the following decision tree, what is the net present value at t=0 of taking branch A?
   a. 43.7
* b. 30.2
   c. 36.8
   d. 27.3
   e. 25.1

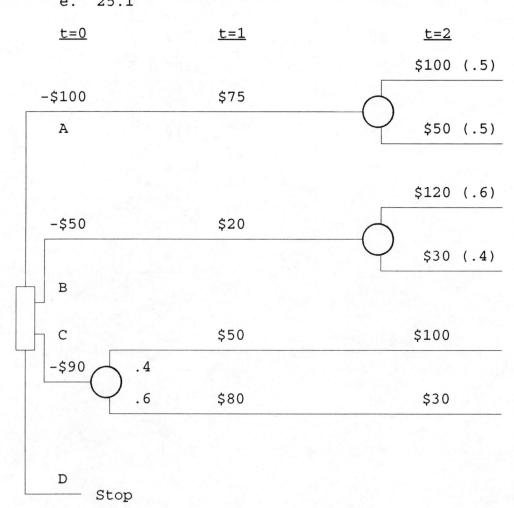

20. Given the following decision tree, what is the net present value at t=0 of taking branch B?
    a. 44.2
    b. 29.5
    c. 39.6
  * d. 37.6
    e. 32.7

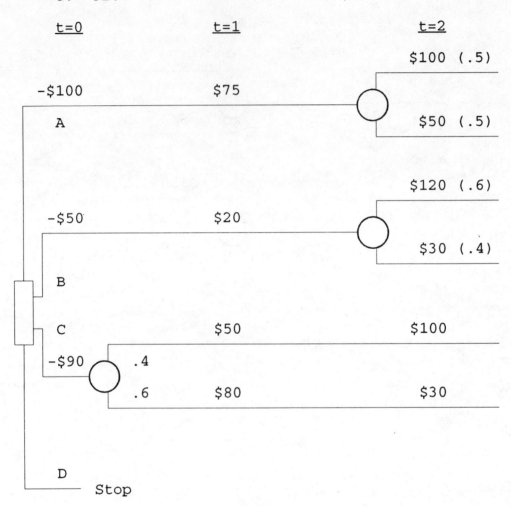

21. Given the following decision tree, what is the net present value at t=0 of taking branch C?
   a. 37.4
   b. 32.7
   c. 19.5
   d. 22.3
* e. 29.5

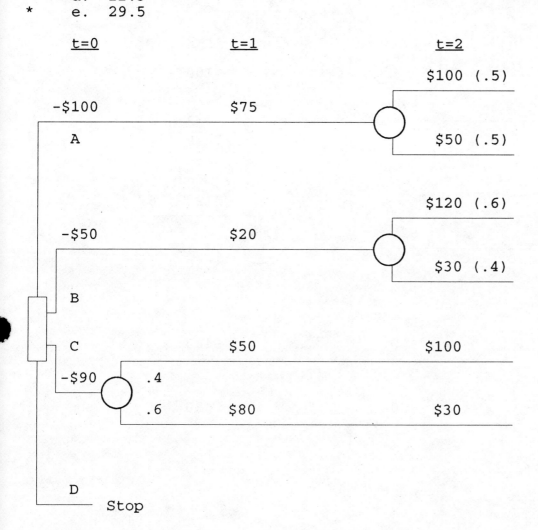

22. Given the following decision tree, which branch should be taken?
    a. Branch A.
 * b. Branch B.
    c. Branch C.
    d. Branch D.

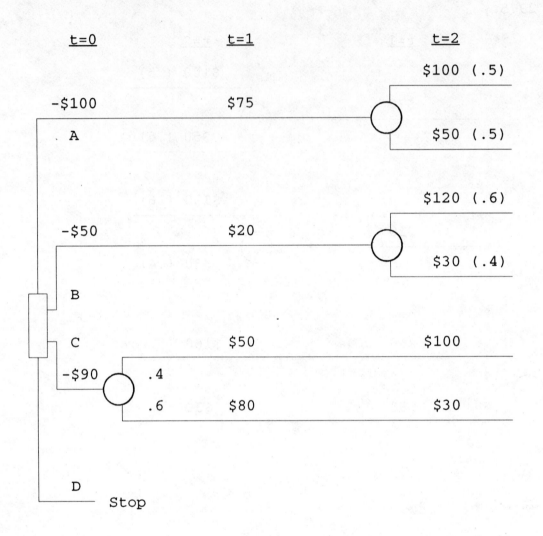

Chapter 10 - True-False Questions

F   1.   As long as a project's risk is wholly diversifiable, a manager does not need to understand why a capital investment project may fail.

T   2.   When conducting a sensitivity analysis, variables are set one at a time to their optimistic and pessimistic values.

T   3.   Sensitivity analysis usually ignores any inter-relationships among underlying variables.

F   4.   Companies can use sensitivity analysis to obtain expected, optimistic, and pessimistic values for total project flows.

T   5.   Companies that break even on an accounting basis are really losing the opportunity cost of capital on their investment.

F   6.   The break-even point in terms of equivalent annual cash flows is usually lower than the break-even point on an accounting basis.

T   7.   By looking at the prospects for a project under alternative scenarios, you can consider the effect of a limited number of plausible combinations of variables.

F   8.   Using sensitivity analysis and analyzing different scenarios is usually better than using net present value.

T   9.   Monte Carlo simulation is a tool for considering all possible combinations of variables.

F   10.   In constructing a simulation model of an investment project, one can ignore possible interdependencies between variables.

F   11.   Some advocates of simulation recommend that it should be used to calculate the project's dispersion of possible NPVs. In this case, the simulated cash flows are discounted at the opportunity cost of capital.

T   12.   In drawing a decision tree, a square represents a decision point for the company, and a circle represents a decision point for fate.

F   13.   In analyzing a decision tree, we begin at the left (i.e., at the beginning) and work our way to the right (i.e., the end).

T   14. Tangible assets usually have a higher abandonment value than intangible ones.

F   15. Ignoring abandonment value usually leads to an overestimate of true project NPV.

T   16. Any cash flow forecast involves some assumption about the firm's future investment and operating strategy. Decision trees help the manager to find the strategy with the highest NPV.

F   17. When drawing a decision tree, it is important to include all possible eventualities.

T   18. If today's decisions affect what you can do tomorrow, then tomorrow's decisions have to be analyzed before you can act rationally today.

F   19. Decision trees are simple and easy to construct.

T   20. Most simulation models incorporate a "business as usual" strategy.

Chapter 10 - Essay Questions

1. Discuss the usefulness of financial decision tools such as sensitivity analysis and Monte Carlo simulation.

Answer
    Sensitivity analysis and Monte Carlo simulation are very useful tools when used properly: Like any tools, they have advantages and limitations. Specifically:
    Sensitivity analysis is a quick and easy way to discover which variables are the critical ones. It requires the manager to identify the underlying variables of interest, indicates where additional information would be most useful, and helps to expose inappropriate forecasts. It does not, however, provide a decision manager with unambiguous results, nor does it take into account interdependencies among different variables.
    Monte Carlo simulation provides a complete picture of the distribution of project outcomes. The problem is that developing the model is time-consuming, expensive, and difficult to verify. And, if the model is wrong, the output - no matter how impressive it looks - is useless. Moreover, the distribution of outcomes does not properly reflect non-diversifiable risk.

2. Discuss break-even analysis.

Answer
    Break-even analysis means the calculation of the point at which a project or product is "in the black," i.e., making money. When used properly, break-even analysis is a useful financial management tool. However, there are two ways break-even is interpreted: In an accounting sense - that is, when does the project become profitable? - and in a net present value sense - that is, when does the project's net present value become positive? Unfortunately, the former is the more common; the latter is the correct way to do the analysis.
    The problem with calculating break-even in the accounting sense is that using profit figures ignores the opportunity cost of capital of the initial investment. For this reason, accounting break-even points are typically lower than those calculated correctly, i.e., calculated using net present value, and may lead managers to invest in projects that have a negative net present value.

Chapter 11 - Multiple Choice Questions

1. As a 19th century economist, you are faced with the following problem. The world shipping fleet consists of 1,200 steamships and 1,200 sailing ships. Each can be used (with minor conversion) to carry cargo or passengers. The ships have similar carrying capacity but differ in terms of their annual operating costs as follows:

	Steam	Sail
Cargo	$80,000	$95,000
Passengers	90,000	100,000

Due to a shortfall in demand, only 1,000 cargo ships and 1,000 passenger ships of either type are required. Assume: (i) fares are competitively determined; (ii) demand is not expected to change; (iii) each vessel has a life of 15 years; (iv) current salvage value of either a steamship or a sailing ship is $114,091; and (v) the cost of capital is 10 percent. What is the present value of a steamship?
* a. $190,152
  b. $215,326
  c. $608,486
  d. None of the above.

2. Look again at Question 1. What is the annual revenue from a cargo ship? (Assume salvage values are independent of use.)
  a. $80,000
* b. $105,000
  c. $115,000
  d. None of the above.

3. Look again at question 1. If the cost of carrying cargo by sailing ship were $75,000 per annum, what would be the present value of a steamship?
* a. $114,091
  b. $152,814
  c. $215,326
  d. None of the above.

4. Demand for concave utility meters is expanding rapidly, but the industry is highly competitive. A utility meter plant costs $50 million to set up and has an annual capacity of 500,000 meters. The production cost is $5 a meter and this cost is not expected to change. If the plant has an indefinite physical life and the cost of capital is 10 percent, what is the price of a utility meter?
    a. $5
    b. $10
*   c. $15
    d. None of the above.

5. Look again at question 4. Suppose that the cost of a new meter plant is now expected to decline in year 2 to $40 million. This is a once-and-for-all decline. Meter plant manufacturers are confident that it will still be worthwhile to install new plants in both years 0 and 1. If they are right, what is the expected price of a utility meter in years 1 and 2?
    a. Year 1 = $10, year 2 = $10
*   b. Year 1 = $35, year 2 = $13
    c. Year 1 = $20, year 2 = $20
    d. Year 1 = $20, year 2 = $30
    e. None of the above.

6. Demand for concave utility meters is expanding rapidly, but the industry is highly competitive. A utility meter plant costs $20 million to set up and has an annual capacity of 100,000 meters. The production cost is $10 a meter, and this cost is not expected to change. If the plant has an indefinite physical life and the cost of capital is 5 percent, what is the price of a utility meter?
*   a. $20
    b. $15
    c. $10
    d. None of the above.

7. Look again at question 6. Suppose that the cost of a new meter plant is now expected to decline in year 2 to $10 million. This is a once-and-for-all decline. Meter plant manufacturers are confident that it will still be worthwhile to install new plants in both years 0 and 1. If they are right, what is the expected price of a utility meter in years 1 and 2?
    a. Year 1 = $100, year 2 = $20
*   b. Year 1 = $120, year 2 = $15
    c. Year 1 = $100, year 2 = $20
    d. Year 1 = $120, year 2 = $15
    e. None of the above.

8. Suppose the current price of gold is $350 per ounce, and your financial advisor estimates that the price of gold will grow at 5 percent per year for the foreseeable future. If the appropriate discount rate is 105, the present value of gold is:
    a. Need more information to decide.
    b. Less than $350 per ounce.
    c. Greater than $350 per ounce.
*   d. $350 per ounce.

9. Which of the following statements is true?
    a. A firm that earns the opportunity cost of capital is earning economic rents.
    b. A firm that earns less than the opportunity cost of capital is earning economic rents.
*   c. Financial managers should try to identify areas where their firm can earn economic rents, because it's there that positive NPV projects are likely to be found.
    d. Economic rent is the equivalent annual cost of operating capital equipment.

10. Which of the following statements is true?
    a. A firm that earns the opportunity cost of capital is earning economic rents.
    b. A firm that invests in zero net present value projects expects to earn economic rents.
    c. Economic rent is the equivalent annual cost of operating capital equipment.
*   d. A firm that invests in positive net present value ventures expects to earn economic rents.

11. You are trying to decide whether to open a new retail store. You can either buy or rent the space. Cash flows in thousands are:

	Initial Investment	Operating flows
Buy	$5,000	$280
Rent	3,000	180

Your real estate advisor thinks that real estate values will increase by 5 percent per year in real terms. All other cash flows, including rents, are expected to remain constant in real terms. The real cost of capital for retail operations is 6.5 percent regardless of whether you buy or rent. Assuming you believe your advisor, you should:
    a. Open the store and buy the retail space.
    b. Open the store and rent the retail space.
*   c. Do nothing.
    d. Need more information to make a decision.

12. Economic rents may arise from:
    a. Production cost advantages.
    b. Proprietary knowledge.
    c. Being first to market a new product.
    * d. All of the above.

13. In order to better understand a proposed positive net present value project, managers should:
    a. Recheck all calculations.
    b. Ensure there are no forecast errors in the calculations.
    * c. Identify the source of the economic rents.
    d. Evaluate other similar projects the company has undertaken in the past.

14. You have inherited 100 acres of Illinois farmland. There is an active market in land of this type, and similar properties are selling for $2,000 per acre. If planted with corn (the crop you are most familiar with), net cash returns are expected to be $180 per acre per year, forever. How much is the land worth, per acre? A local consultant has advised using a discount rate of 10%.
    a. More than $2,000.
    * b. $2,000.
    c. $1,800.
    d. Less than $1,800.

15. You have inherited a run-down house in Boston. There is an active market in properties of this type, and similar properties are selling for $60,000. If rented out, net cash returns are expected to be $8,400 per year, forever. How much is the house worth? A local consultant has advised using a discount rate of 15%.
    * a. $60,000.
    b. More than $60,000.
    c. $56,000.
    d. Less than $56,000.

16. You have inherited a trailer. There is an active market in equipment of this type, and similar items are selling for $5,000. If rented out, net cash returns are expected to be $500 per year, forever. How much is the trailer worth? A local consultant has advised using a discount rate of 12%.
    a. $4,167.
    b. Less than $4,167.
    c. More than $5,000.
    * d. $5,000.

17. You have inherited a run-down house in Atlanta. There is an active market in properties of this type, and similar properties are selling for $80,000. You are quite skilled in repair work and already have several rental units; if the newly acquired property is rented out, net cash returns are expected to be $13,000 per year, forever. How much is the house worth? A local consultant has advised using a discount rate of 15%.
    a. $80,000.
    b. $73,667.
    c. Less than $73,667.
*   d. More than $80,000.

18. The manufacture of frolic acid is a competitive industry. Plants have an annual output of 100,000 tons. Operating costs are 50 cents per ton. A 100,000 ton plant costs $500,000 to build and has an indefinite life, with no scrap value. The cost of capital is 20%; assume no taxes.
    Your company has discovered a new process that lowers the cost per ton to 40 cents. Assuming the competition will never catch up and that market demand is sufficiently high, what is the net present value of building one new plant with the new technology?
*   a. $50,000.
    b. $100,000.
    c. $250,000.
    d. $550,000.

19. The manufacture of frolic acid is a competitive industry. Plants have an annual output of 100,000 tons. Operating costs are 50 cents per ton. A 100,000 ton plant costs $500,000 to build and has an indefinite life, with no scrap value. The cost of capital is 20%; assume no taxes.
    Your company has discovered a new process that lowers the cost per ton to 40 cents. Assuming that market demand is sufficiently high and that the competition will catch up in two years, what is the net present value of building one plant with the new technology?
    a. Zero.
    b. $68,056.
*   c. $15,278.
    d. $10,000.

20. The manufacture of frolic acid is a competitive industry. Plants have an annual output of 100,000 tons. Operating costs are 50 cents per ton. A 100,000 ton plant costs $500,000 to build and has an indefinite life, with no scrap value. The cost of capital is 20%; assume no taxes.

Your company has discovered a new process that lowers the cost per ton to 40 cents. Assuming that market demand is sufficiently high and that the competition will catch up in four years, what is the net present value of building one plant with the new technology?
    a.   Zero.
*   b. $25,887.
    c. $17,344.
    d. $15,000.

Chapter 11 - True-False Questions

F   1. Sometimes the financial manager can observe market values for real assets, e.g., real estate values, prices of second-hand airplanes, values of precious metals, etc. However, these values have no place in capital investment analysis. For that purpose discounted cash flow is the only proper tool.

T   2. A manager considering the acquisition of a specific asset should begin with the market price of that asset and then ask why the asset will earn more if used by his/her company than it will if used by rival companies.

F   3. If an asset is worth more to others than it is to you, you should always attempt to buy it from them.

T   4. Since gold is held as an investment but pays no cash dividends, today's price equals the present value of its forecasted future price.

F   5. If an asset pays no dividends, is traded in a competitive market, and costs nothing to store, then the current price is less than the discounted value of the future price.

T   6. If others are producing a product profitably and you can make it at a lower cost, your net present value will be positive.

F   7. Forecast errors for cash flows from different projects are not a serious concern as long as the average error across all the forecasts is zero.

T   8. When an industry settles into long-run competitive equilibrium, all its assets are expected to earn their respective opportunity costs of capital.

F   9. In order to generate a positive net present value project, a company must have a short-run competitive advantage.

T   10. A positive net present value project is believable only if you believe your company has some special advantage.

F   11. The NPV of an investment is less than the discounted value of the economic rents that it is expected to produce.

T   12. The NPV of an investment is the discounted value of the economic rents that it is expected to produce.

F   13. To increase shareholder wealth, a firm should scrap equipment whenever the present value of the future cash flows is less than the value of the written-down investment.

T   14. In evaluating a project, it is necessary to consider its effect upon the sales of the firm's existing products.

F   15. If a firm must work with biased cash flow forecasts, it is generally better to use the payback rule rather than net present value.

T   16. If a company anticipates long-run economic rents from a particular project, the company is probably ignoring the effects of competition.

F   17. A manager should not assume that economic rents will continue indefinitely: When other firms gain access to the same opportunities that his/her firm has, the internal rate of return of his/her equipment will be forced down to zero.

T   18. A company can expect to earn economic rents only if it has some superior resource such as management, sales force, design team, production facilities, etc.

F   19. The net present value of a new item of equipment is increased if the salvage value of existing competitive equipment is decreased.

T   20. Many firms begin the capital budgeting process by establishing forecasts of economic indicators. This helps to ensure that forecasts are based on consistent assumptions.

Chapter 11 - Essay Questions

1. Discuss the possible sources of economic rents. Why are economic rents important to a manager?

<u>Answer</u>

Economic rents are important because they are the source of positive net present values. Economic rents can arise from a variety of sources, but fundamentally reflect a company's competitive advantages, whether in being first to market a product or having lower production costs, proprietary knowledge, patent protection, some contractual advantage, etc.

2. Discuss how you would react if you were presented with a project that had a positive net present value.

<u>Answer</u>

The basic question is, why is the net present value positive? Is it because of some forecast error, because market values were ignored, or because the project genuinely exploits the company's competitive advantages and thus generates economic rents? You should proceed with the project only if you are satisfied that you understand the source of the economic rents that are implied by the positive net present value.

Chapter 12 - Multiple Choice Questions

1. Which of the following statements regarding appropriation requests is true?
   a. Usually submitted by head office staff.
   b. Represents the first step in the capital budgeting process.
   * c. Authorization tends to be reserved for senior management.
   d. None of the above.

2. Which of the following statements regarding appropriation requests is true?
   a. Usually submitted by head office staff.
   * b. Usually require the calculation of more than one investment criterion.
   c. Usually subjected to a single review at the head office.
   d. None of the above.

3. Which of the following are typical categories of capital budgeting projects?
   a. Safety or environmental outlays.
   b. Maintenance or cost reduction.
   c. Capacity expansion.
   d. New products.
   * e. All of the above.

4. Which of the following types of projects would not have to satisfy a strict positive net present value rule?
   * a. Safety or environmental outlays.
   b. Maintenance or cost reduction.
   c. Capacity expansion.
   d. New products.
   e. None of the above.

5. Which of the following types of projects would depend most on intangible considerations?
   a. Safety or environmental outlays.
   b. Maintenance or cost reduction.
   c. Capacity expansion.
   * d. New products.
   e. None of the above.

6. Typical problems in capital budgeting include which of the following?
   a. Ensuring that forecasts are accurate.
   b. Eliminating conflicts of interest.
   c. Reducing forecast bias.
   d. Recognizing strategic fit.
   * e. All of the above.

7. If top management increases its estimate of the opportunity cost of capital from 10% to 15%, Brealey & Myers's Second Law suggests that the proportion of proposed projects with a positive NPV will:
   * a. Remain the same.
   b. Decrease by 50%.
   c. Decrease by less than 50%.
   d. Increase.

8. A postaudit will:
   a. Identify problems that need to be fixed.
   b. Check the accuracy of cash flow forecasts.
   c. Suggest questions that should have been asked before the project was undertaken.
   * d. All of the above.

9. Which of the following controls is usually imposed on capital projects?
   a. Company requires revised appropriation request if there is a significant change in the nature of the project.
   b. Company requires the sponsor to submit a formal notice of completion.
   c. Company requires a new appropriation request for any projects that are not completed by the year-end.
   d. Company requires monthly or quarterly status reports on project.
   * e. All of the above.

10. Other things equal, which of the following conditions is usually associated with a high *book* rate of return? Assume an ongoing business in a "steady state" of growth.
    * a. Heavy investment in intangibles, e.g., R&D.
    b. Rapid growth.
    c. Straight-line book depreciation.
    d. Rapid technical change, so that costs decline rapidly over time.
    e. None of the above.

11. Other things equal, which of the following conditions is usually associated with a high *book* rate of return? Assume an ongoing business in a "steady state" of growth.
      a. Rapid growth.
*   b. Accelerated book depreciation.
      d. Short start-up or break-in periods before new assets become fully productive.
      d. Rapid technical change, so that costs decline rapidly over time.
      e. None of the above.

12. Other things equal, which of the following conditions is usually associated with a high *book* rate of return? Assume an ongoing business in a "steady state" of growth.
      a. No investment in intangibles, e.g., R&D.
      b. Rapid growth.
      c. Straight line book depreciation.
*   d. Extended start-up or break-in periods before new assets become fully productive.
      e. Rapid technical change, so that costs decline rapidly over time.

13. What is the definition of the economic rate of return?
      a. $[C_{t+1} + PV_{t+1}] / PV_t$

*   b. $[C_{t+1} + (PV_{t+1} - PV_t)] / PV_t$

      c. $[PV_{t+1}] / PV_t$

      d. None of the above.

14. For a company growing at a steady rate, book return on investment (ROI) will equal the true (economic) rate of return if:
      a. The amount that the firm invests each year grows at a rate higher than the true rate.
      b. The amount that the firm invests each year grows at a rate lower than the true rate.
*   c. The amount that the firm invests each year grows at a rate equal to the true rate.

15. Consider an asset with the following cash flows:

Year: 0 1 2 3
Cash Flow,
  millions of $:   -21.0   9.1   8.4   7.7

The firm uses straight-line book depreciation. Thus, for this project, it writes off $7 per year in years 1, 2, and 3. The discount rate is 10%.

Economic depreciation in years 1, 2, and 3 is:
    a. 9, 7, and 5.
    b. 5, 7, and 9.
*   c. 7, 7, and 7.
    d. None of the above.

16. Consider an asset with the following cash flows:

Year: 0 1 2 3
Cash Flow,
  millions of $:   -21.0   9.1   8.4   7.7

The firm uses straight-line book depreciation. Thus, for this project, it writes off $7 per year in years 1, 2, and 3. The discount rate is 10%.

Economic income in years 1, 2, and 3 is:
*   a. 2.1, 1.4, and 0.7.
    b. 9.1, 8.4, and 0.7.
    c. 8.4, 8.4, and 8.4.
    d. None of the above.

17. Consider an asset with the following cash flows:

Year: 0 1 2 3
Cash Flow,
  millions of $:   -40.0   29.0   11.5   5.5

The firm uses straight-line book depreciation. Thus, for this project, it writes off $13.3 per year in years 1, 2, and 3. The discount rate is 10%.

Economic depreciation in years 1, 2, and 3 is:
    a. 13.3, 13.3, and 13.3.
*   b. 25, 10, and 5.
    c. 20, 10, and 10.
    d. None of the above.

18. Consider an asset with the following cash flows:

Year: 0   1   2   3
Cash Flow,
  millions of $:   -40.0   29.0   11.5   5.5

The firm uses straight-line book depreciation. Thus, for this project, it writes off $13.3 per year in years 1, 2, and 3. The discount rate is 10%.

Economic income in years 1, 2, and 3 is:
    a.   2.0, 2.0, and 2.0.
    b.   15.7, -1.8, and -7.8.
*   c.   4.0, 1.5, and 0.5.
    d.   None of the above.

19. Consider an asset with the following cash flows:

Year: 0   1   2   3
Cash Flow,
  millions of $:   -40.0   29.0   11.5   5.5

The firm uses straight-line book depreciation. Thus, for this project, it writes off $13.3 per year in years 1, 2, and 3. The discount rate is 10%.

The economic rate of return in years 1, 2, and 3 is:
*   a.   .100, .100, and .100.
    b.   .393, -.067, and -.586.
    c.   .725, .397, and .478.
    d.   None of the above.

20. Consider an asset with the following cash flows:

Year: 0   1   2   3
Cash Flow,
  millions of $:   -30.0   16.0   19.0   6.0

The firm uses straight-line book depreciation. Thus, for this project, it writes off $10 per year in years 1, 2, and 3. The discount rate is 20%.

Economic depreciation in years 1, 2, and 3 is:
    a.   10, 10, and 10.
    b.   15, 10, and 5.
*   c.   10, 15, and 5.
    d.   None of the above.

21. Consider an asset with the following cash flows:

Year:	0	1	2	3
Cash Flow, millions of $:	-30.0	16.0	19.0	6.0

The firm uses straight-line book depreciation. Thus, for this project, it writes off $10 per year in years 1, 2, and 3. The discount rate is 20%.

Economic income in years 1, 2, and 3 is:
    a. 13.7, 13.7, and 13.7.
*   b.   6.0, 4.0, and 1.0.
    c.   3.7, 3.7, and 3.7.
    d. None of the above.

Chapter 12 - True-False Questions

T   1. The annual capital budget contains a list of proposed new projects for the coming year and any projects from earlier years that are incomplete.

F   2. The approval of the capital budget generally confers authority to undertake the projects listed in the budget.

T   3. If a company uses an annual capital budget process, one danger is a loss of flexibility: it may be difficult to get approval for a project during the year.

F   4. Because of the large number of investment proposals, most companies delegate to the plant manager the authority to approve substantial items of capital expenditure.

T   5. In many firms, the capital budget contains rough estimates of likely expenditures over a five-year period.

F   6. Most companies consider only two categories of capital projects, cost reduction and capacity expansion.

T   7. The decision to proceed with a new product would depend heavily on intangible considerations.

F   8. All projects must "pay their own way," that is, must have a positive net present value.

T   9. Appropriation requests are typically prepared by the project originator but submitted by the plant manager.

F   10. The majority of companies uses only one criterion when appraising capital expenditures.

T   11. Many companies begin the capital budgeting process by forecasting key economic indicators, such as inflation and growth in national income.

F   12. Brealey & Myers's Second Law states that the proportion of proposed projects having a positive NPV decreases as top management's estimate of the opportunity cost of capital increases.

T   13. Capital rationing may be used by firms to decentralize investment decisions.

F   14. Capital rationing does not require operating managers to set priorities.

T   15. If cash flow forecasts are not unbiased, *ad hoc* capital budgeting procedures may yield better decisions than net present value.

F   16. A postaudit should be performed on every capital budgeting project.

T   17. The most common time for a postaudit of an investment project is one year after installation.

F   18. Typically, a company will require a supplemental appropriation request for all cost overruns, regardless of the amount.

T   19. Often postaudits cannot measure all cash flows generated by a project.

F   20. Firms which use accelerated depreciation will consistently report lower book rates of return than firms which use straight-line depreciation.

T   21. Firms which make heavy investments in R&D and other intangible assets will generally report book rates of return which overstate true returns.

F   22. Errors in performance measurement from using book depreciation will cancel out in the long run.

T   23. Economic income = cash flow + change in present value.

F   24. Book income = cash flow + book depreciation.

T   25. Economic return on an investment differs from book return if the reduction in the present value of the asset is not the same as the book depreciation.

Chapter 12 - Essay Questions

1. Discuss the problems inherent in any capital budgeting process.

<u>Answer</u>

The key problems are:
  1. Ensuring that forecasts are consistent. This requires that some baseline of expected economic conditions is agreed on and used by all those involved in the forecasting of cash flows.
  2. Eliminating conflicts of interest. The problem here is to ensure that a manager's performance is evaluated and rewarded in a manner consistent with increasing net present value, the goal of the capital budgeting process. If this is not the case - if rewards, for example, are based on size or book return or some other criterion - then capital budgeting decisions will also be made according to those criteria, not NPV.
  3. Reducing forecast bias. Project supporters are likely to be overly optimistic regarding the cash flow forecasts.
  4. Getting senior management the information it needs. The problem here is that, in large companies, senior management will not see projects until everyone else has already agreed these projects should be accepted. In other words, in large companies, senior management is not involved until too late - the decisions have already been made, for all practical purposes.
  5. Recognizing strategic fit. Just because a project has a positive net present value does not automatically mean it should be accepted. Other considerations - e.g., does this project fit with our company's competitive advantage? - are also important.

2. Discuss the importance of conducting postaudits.

<u>Answer</u>

Postaudits are important for several reasons. First, they identify problems in the capital budgeting process that should be fixed. Second, they provide a check on the accuracy of the cash flow forecasts used, although sometimes it can be hard to separate the effects of judgment from sheer luck (that is, it can be hard to tell the difference between bad forecasts and better-than-expected economic conditions and good forecasts and worse-than-expected economic conditions). Third, they raise questions that, in retrospect, should have been asked about the project before it was undertaken. Postaudits are also expensive, in terms of the people-time required, and so they are typically used only for selected large projects.

Chapter 13 - Multiple Choice Questions

1. If capital markets are efficient, then the purchase or sale of any security at the prevailing market price:
   a. Is always a positive-NPV transaction.
   b. Is always a negative-NPV transaction.
   * c. Is never a positive-NPV transaction.
   d. Is never a negative-NPV transaction.

2. Which of the following would be of interest to a fundamental analyst?
   * a. Information about a new product under development.
   b. Recent stock price behavior.
   c. The relationship between the stock price and the S&P 500.
   d. None of the above.

3. Suppose that, after conducting an analysis of past stock prices, you came up with the following observations. Which would appear to contradict the weak form of the efficient market hypothesis?
   a. The average return is significantly greater than zero.
   * b. The correlation between the return one week and the return the next week is -.3.
   c. The correlation between the return one week and the return the next week is 0.
   d. One could have made higher than average capital gains by holding shares with low dividend yields.

4. Suppose that, after conducting an analysis of past stock prices, you came up with the following observations. Which would appear to contradict the weak form of the efficient market hypothesis?
   a. The average return is significantly greater than zero.
   b. The correlation between the return one week and the return the next week is 0.
   * c. One could have made superior returns by buying stock after a 10 percent rise in price and selling after a 10 percent fall.
   d. One could have made higher-than-average capital gains by holding shares with low dividend yields.

5. Which of the following statements is/are true if the efficient market hypothesis holds?
   a. It implies perfect forecasting ability.
   b. It implies that the market is irrational.
   c. It implies that prices do not fluctuate.
* d. It implies that prices reflect all available information.
   e. None of the above.

6. Which of the following observations would provide evidence against the strong form of the efficient market theory?
   a. Mutual fund managers do not on average make superior returns.
   b. You cannot make superior profits by buying (or selling) stocks after the announcement of an abnormal rise in earnings.
   c. In any year approximately 50 percent of all pension funds outperform the market.
* d. Managers who trade in their own stocks make superior returns.
   e. None of the above.

7. Which of the following observations would provide evidence against the strong form of the efficient market theory?
* a. You can make superior profits by buying stocks before the announcement of an abnormal rise in earnings.
   b. You cannot make superior profits by buying (or selling) stocks after the announcement of an abnormal rise in earnings.
   c. Mutual fund managers do not on average make superior returns.
   d. In any year approximately 50 percent of all pension funds outperform the market.
   e. None of the above.

8. Financing decisions differ from investment decisions for which of the following reasons?
   a. You can't use NPV to evaluate financing decisions.
* b. The market for financial assets is more active and extensive than for real assets.
   c. It's easier to find positive-NPV financing decisions than to find positive-NPV investment decisions.
   d. None of the above.

9. Financing decisions differ from investment decisions for which of the following reasons?
    a. You can't use NPV to evaluate financing decisions.
    b. It's easier to find positive-NPV financing decisions than to find positive-NPV investment decisions.
*   c. Real asset markets are typically less efficient than markets for financial assets.
    d. None of the above.

10. Historically, the gains made by mutual fund managers:
*   a. Are just about enough to cover the expenses of managing the portfolios.
    b. Are significantly more than the expenses of managing the portfolios.
    c. Are significantly less than the expenses of managing the portfolios.

11. The Crash of 1987 was caused by:
    a. Index arbitragers.
    b. Institutional investors using portfolio insurance techniques.
    c. Small investors.
*   d. None of the above.

12. In an efficient market, managers should issue more common stock:
    a. When additional equity financing is required and after a period of time during which the price of the company's stock has increased.
    b. When additional equity financing is required and after a period of time during which the price of the company's stock has decreased.
    c. When additional equity financing is required and after a period of time during which the price of the company's stock has been about the same.
*   d. When additional equity financing is required.

13. In an efficient market, if a stock is selling for $200 per share and it is split 2:1, the new shares will sell for:
    a. A little less than $100 per share.
*   b. A little more than $100 per share.
    c. Exactly $100 per share.

14. In an efficient market:
   a. Publicly held companies should diversify their operations because investors benefit from diversification.
* b. Publicly held companies should not diversify their operations.
   c. Investors do not care whether or not companies diversify their operations.
   d. None of the above.

15. Analysis of past monthly movements in Pillsbury's stock price produces the following estimates:

   α = 1.65 percent and β = .6

If the market index subsequently rises by 8 percent in one month and Pillsbury's stock price rises by 7 percent, what is the abnormal change in Pillsbury's stock price?
   a. -3.65 percent.
   b. -1.00 percent.
* c. + .55 percent.
   d. +2.65 percent.

16. Analysis of past monthly movements in IBM's stock price produces the following estimates:

   α = .75 percent and β = .9

If the market index subsequently rises by 10 percent in one month and IBM's stock price rises by 12 percent, what is the abnormal change in IBM's stock price?
* a. +2.25 percent.
   b. +3.00 percent.
   c. -2.25 percent.
   d. -1.00 percent.

17. Analysis of past monthly movements in AT&T's stock price produces the following estimates:

   α = -.45 percent and β = .5

If the market index subsequently rises by 5 percent in one month and AT&T's stock price rises by 3 percent, what is the abnormal change in AT&T's stock price?
   a. +.05 percent.
   b. -.95 percent.
   c. -.05 percent.
* d. +.95 percent.

18. Analysis of past monthly movements in Microsoft's stock price produces the following estimates:

$$\alpha = 2.50 \text{ percent} \quad \text{and} \quad \beta = 1.6$$

If the market index subsequently rises by 12 percent in one month and Microsoft's stock price rises by 20 percent, what is the abnormal change in Microsoft's stock price?
    a.   - .8 percent.
*   b.   -1.7 percent.
    c.   -8.0 percent.
    d.   + .8 percent.

19. Analysis of past monthly movements in Trico's stock price produces the following estimates:

$$\alpha = .25 \text{ percent} \quad \text{and} \quad \beta = 2.4$$

If the market index subsequently rises by 15 percent in one month and Trico's stock price rises by 25 percent, what is the abnormal change in Trico's stock price?
    a.   - 1.25 percent.
*   b.   -11.25 percent.
    c.   +10.00 percent.
    d.   +11.00 percent.

20. Analysis of past monthly movements in Wells Fargo's stock price produces the following estimates:

$$\alpha = .35 \text{ percent} \quad \text{and} \quad \beta = 1.3$$

If the market index subsequently rises by 4 percent in one month and Wells Fargo's stock price rises by 6 percent, what is the abnormal change in Wells Fargo's stock price?
    a.   +2.00 percent.
    b.   - .45 percent.
*   c.   + .45 percent.
    d.   + .80 percent.

Chapter 13 - True-False Questions

T   1. A good financing decision is one in which the amount of cash raised exceeds the value of the liability created.

F   2. Financing decisions cannot be analyzed according to the net present value rule.

T   3. For a corporation, financing decisions are usually easier to reverse than investment decisions.

F   4. In an efficient market, information is free.

T   5. Firms should assume that the securities they issue are fairly priced by the capital market.

F   6. In an efficient market, stock prices follow established patterns.

T   7. If capital markets are efficient, then the purchase or sale of any security at the prevailing market price is never a positive-NPV transaction.

F   8. The true value of a security is its ultimate future value.

T   9. Security prices that follow a random walk are characteristic of a competitive market.

F   10. The way to make money in the stock market is to identify the cycles followed by stocks and trade according to these cycles.

T   11. As soon as a cycle becomes apparent to investors, they immediately eliminate it by their trading.

F   12. There is considerable evidence that successive share price changes are highly correlated.

T   13. The weak form of the efficient market theory implies that security prices reflect all the information contained in past security prices.

F   14. The weak form of the efficient market theory implies that technical analysis is valuable.

T   15. The weak form of the efficient market theory implies that security prices follow a random walk.

F   16.   The gains made by professional mutual fund managers more than make up for the expenses of managing the portfolios.

T   17.   If the strong form of the efficient market theory is correct, the weak form of the theory must also be correct. The reverse is not true.

F   18.   The evidence suggests that, although many professionally managed funds do consistently outperform the market, the average fund does not do so.

T   19.   In an efficient market, you can trust market prices because they impound all available information.

F   20.   Abnormal return = actual return + expected return.

T   21.   "Creative accounting" refers to the practice of choosing accounting methods which stabilize and increase reported earnings.

F   22.   Stock splits are good for investors because they increase investors' cash flow.

T   23.   In an efficient market, investors will not pay others for what they can do equally well themselves.

F   24.   If other investors agree that you do not have some private information, you cannot sell large quantities of common stock at close to the market price.

Chapter 13 - Essay Questions

1. Explain why, in a competitive securities market, successive price changes will be random.

Answer

In a competitive market, prices will incorporate, or reflect, all available information. This must be so, or else the market is ignoring some important information, which cannot happen if competition is sufficiently strong. It follows that prices will change only when new information arrives. But, by definition, new information arrives randomly: After all, if we could predict its arrival, when it in fact arrived, it would not be new. So, prices react to new information, and new information arrives randomly - so successive price changes are random.

2. Sometimes managers prefer to issue common stock after their stock price has risen. Does this make sense in an efficient market?

Answer

No, because the managers are in effect trying to catch the market while it is high. The implicit assumption is that security market prices move in cycles, and hence it is advantageous to issue when the price is at the peak of its cycle. If the market is efficient, markets have no memory, and security prices do not move in cycles.

Chapter 14 - Multiple Choice Questions

1. The book value of Placebo Drug Company's common equity is as follows:

Common shares ($.50 par value)	$1,000,000
Additional paid-in capital	4,000,000
Retained earnings	5,500,000
Treasury shares, at cost	(200,000)
Net common equity	$10,300,000

Suppose that the company now sells 500,000 additional shares at a price of $2.25 each. What is the new value for common shares?
    a. $1,000,000
    b. $2,125,000
*   c. $1,250,000
    d. $4,500,000
    e. None of the above.

2. The book value of Placebo Drug Company's common equity is as follows:

Common shares ($.50 par value)	$1,000,000
Additional paid-in capital	4,000,000
Retained earnings	5,500,000
Treasury shares, at cost	(200,000)
Net common equity	$10,300,000

Suppose that the company now sells 500,000 additional shares at a price of $2.25 each. What is the new value for additional paid-in capital?
*   a. $4,875,000
    b. $4,625,000
    c. $4,000,000
    d. $5,125,000
    e. None of the above.

3. The book value of How Corp.'s common equity is as follows:

Common shares ($.25 par value)	$2,000,000
Additional paid-in capital	1,000,000
Retained earnings	4,000,000
Net common equity	$7,000,000

Suppose that the company now sells 1,000,000 additional shares at a price of $4.25 each. What is the new value for common shares?
    a. $4,000,000
    b. $3,000,000
    c. $6,250,000
    d. $2,000,000
*   e. None of the above.

4. The book value of How Corp.'s common equity is as follows:
   Common shares ($.25 par value) $2,000,000
   Additional paid-in capital   1,000,000
   Retained earnings   4,000,000
   Net common equity $7,000,000

Suppose that the company now sells 1,000,000 additional shares at a price of $4.25 each. What is the new value for additional paid-in capital?
   a. $5,250,000
 * b. $5,000,000
   c. $3,000,000
   d. $1,000,000
   e. None of the above.

5. The book value of How Corp.'s common equity is as follows:
   Common shares ($.25 par value) $2,000,000
   Additional paid-in capital   1,000,000
   Retained earnings   4,000,000
   Net common equity $7,000,000

What is the market value of How's common stock?
   a. $2,000,000
   b. $1,000,000
   c. $3,000,000
   d. $7,000,000
 * e. Need more information.

6. You have 100 shares and there are five directors to be elected. Under majority voting, what is the maximum number of votes you can cast for any candidate?
   a. One.
   b. Five.
 * c. One hundred.
   d. Five hundred.
   e. None of the above.

7. You have 100 shares and there are five directors to be elected. Under cumulative voting, what is the maximum number of votes you can cast for any candidate?
   a. One.
   b. Five.
   c. One hundred.
 * d. Five hundred.
   e. None of the above.

8. Which of the following items involves a contradiction?
* a. An unsecured mortgage bond.
   b. Cumulative preferred stock.
   c. A subordinated debenture.
   d. A floating rate loan paying interest at 1 percent above prime.
   e. None of the above.

9. Which of the following items involves a contradiction?
   a. Long-term bond with a sinking fund.
* b. An unfunded 5-year note.
   c. A subordinated debenture.
   d. A floating-rate loan paying interest at 1 percent above LIBOR.
   e. None of the above.

10. Which of the following items involves a contradiction?
   a. Convertible bond with call provision.
   b. A subordinated debenture.
   c. A floating-rate loan paying interest at 1 percent above LIBOR.
* d. A domestic U.S. eurodollar loan.
   e. None of the above.

11. Which of the following statements describes preferred stock?
   a. Offers a fixed dividend.
   b. Dividend is usually at the discretion of directors.
   c. Dividends may not be paid on common unless they are also paid on preferred.
* d. All of the above.
   e. None of the above.

12. Which of the following statements describes preferred stock?
* a. Only 30 percent of dividend is taxable to a corporate holder.
   b. Usually matures in 15 to 20 years.
   c. Confers same voting privileges as common stock.
   d. Preferred dividends are an allowable deduction for corporate income tax.
   e. None of the above.

13. A convertible bond provides an option to change the bond for shares of common stock. Who decides if and when this happens?
   a. The company.
* b. The owner of the convertible bond.
   c. The bond registrar.
   d. None of the above.

14. Which of the following is not a derivative?
    a. Currency swap.
    b. Traded option.
  * c. Preferred stock.
    d. Futures contract.
    e. None of the above.

15. If you wanted to buy a commodity at some point in the future and you wanted to fix the date and price today, you would use:
  * a. Futures contract.
    b. Traded option.
    c. Preferred stock.
    d. Currency swap.
    e. None of the above.

16. On average, what proportion of corporations' sources of cash is generated internally?
    a. About 10 percent.
    b. About 30 percent.
  * c. About 70 percent.
    d. Almost 100 percent.

17. Aggregate statistics on U.S. nonfinancial corporations reveal that since the 1950s the average debt ratio has:
    a. Decreased.
  * b. Increased.
    c. Remained about the same.
    d. Increased, then sharply decreased.

18. In general, since the 1950s firms have covered their financial deficits by:
    a. Issuing preferred stock.
    b. Issuing common stock.
    c. Issuing warrants.
  * d. Issuing debt.
    e. None of the above.

19. The system of corporate governance in the United States is broadly similar to that used in:
  * a. Canada.
    b. Germany.
    c. Japan.
    d. All of the above.
    e. None of the above.

20. Hostile takeovers are common in:
    a. Germany.
    b. Japan.
*   c. The United States.
    d. All of the above.
    e. None of the above.

21. Cross-holdings are common in which systems of corporate governance?
    a. Germany.
    b. Japan.
    c. The United States.
*   d. Germany and Japan.
    e. Germany, Japan and the United States.

Chapter 14 - True-False Questions

T   1.   The maximum number of shares that can be issued is known as the authorized share capital.

F   2.   Most of the issued shares are held by investors. These shares are said to be issued but not outstanding.

T   3.   Under majority voting, each director is voted upon separately.

F   4.   Majority voting makes it easier for a particular group of stockholders to elect a director that will represent that group's interests.

T   5.   A real estate investment trust (REIT) is tightly restricted to real estate investment.

F   6.   The company's debtholders have a general preemptive right to anything of value that the company may wish to distribute.

T   7.   Debt due in less than one year is known as unfunded debt.

F   8.   A floating-rate loan is the opposite of a sinking-fund loan.

T   9.   Many long-term bonds are repaid by means of a sinking fund. In this case, the firm pays a sum of cash each year into a sinking fund which is then used to repurchase the bonds.

F   10. Dividends cannot be paid on preferred stock unless they are also paid on the common stock.

T   11. A subordinated lender holds a junior claim and is, therefore, paid only after all senior creditors are satisfied.

F   12. Investment grade issues account for the majority of trading in the junk bond market.

T   13. If a bond is secured by a mortgage on plant and equipment, the bondholders have first claim on that plant and equipment; other creditors have a general claim on the unmortgaged assets but only a junior claim on the mortgaged assets.

F   14. If the company goes out of business, the preferred stock is junior to both debt and common stock.

T   15. The interest rate the bank charges on loans to its most creditworthy customers is frequently below the prime rate.

F   16. A warrant gives the company the option to sell a set number of common shares at a set price on or before a set date.

T   17. When the owners of a convertible bond wish to exercise their option to buy shares, they do not pay cash - they give up the bond.

F   18. Currency swaps can be used to give the company the right, but not the obligation, to purchase a particular asset in the future at a price that is fixed today.

T   19. A futures contract is an order that is placed in advance to buy or sell an asset or commodity.

F   20. Since 1960 the average book debt ratio for U.S. companies has remained essentially the same.

T   21. Internally generated cash normally covers a majority of firms' capital requirements.

F   22. The system of corporate governance is roughly similar in the United States, Germany, and Japan.

T   23. In most years, companies in general have incurred a financial deficit.

F   24. Hostile corporate takeovers are quite common in Germany.

T   25. A kiretsu is a network of companies, usually organized around a major bank.

Chapter 14 - Essay Questions

1. Discuss, under the United States' system of corporate governance, how the agency problems caused by a separation of ownership and control are mitigated.

Answer

There are several aspects of the U.S. system of corporate governance which can be used to offset agency costs caused by the separation of ownership and control. First, there is a legal duty for these managers to act in the best interests of the shareholders; if they fail to do so, they may be sued. Second, financial incentives for top management are usually tied to the performance of the stock price; if these managers do not act in the best interest of the shareholders, the stock price will fall and their own financial position will be hurt. Third, if these managers fail to act in the best interests of stockholders and the stock price falls, the company may become a takeover target; upon such a takeover, top management is typically replaced.

2. Discuss the differences between the systems of corporate governance used in the United States and in Germany.

Answer

In the U.S. system, ownership is very widely dispersed; that is, for any particular company there are many owners, each of whom holds a very small percentage of the ownership. Thus there is a very high degree of separation of ownership and control: Individual owners have essentially no voice in actually operating the company. In Germany, by way of contrast, ownership is typically concentrated in large blocks which are held by other companies, banks, or families of banks. Thus the degree of separation of ownership and control is much less in Germany as compared to the U.S.

Chapter 15 - Multiple Choice Questions

1. Which of the following statements characterizes the venture capital market?
* a. Venture capital money is advanced in stages. Many startups go through several stages before their IPO.
  b. Venture capital money comes almost entirely from wealthy individuals.
  c. Venture capitalists almost always require a majority of seats on the startup company's board of directors.
  d. None of the above.

2. Which of the following statements characterizes the venture capital market?
  a. Venture capital typically provides zero-stage financing.
  b. Most venture capital comes from corporations.
* c. Venture capital partnerships in the U.S. have recently attracted approximately three billion dollars per year.
  d. None of the above.

3. Which issues do not require registration with the SEC?
  a. Rights issues.
  b. Bonds.
  c. Negotiated offerings by utility holding companies.
* d. Loans maturing within 9 months.
  e. None of the above.

4. Which issues do not require registration with the SEC?
  a. Common stock.
* b. Stock purchased by a venture capitalist from a startup company.
  c. Negotiated offerings by utility holding companies.
  d. Loans maturing within 12 months.
  e. None of the above.

5. Issue costs, including any underpricing, are likely to be higher for:
* a. Initial Public Offerings (vs. seasoned equity issues).
  b. Debt (vs. equity) issues.
  c. Rights issues (vs. general cash offers).

6. Which of the following statements describes shelf registration?
    a. Securities must be issued within a short period of time.
*   b. Allows issues to be made at short notice.
    c. Reduces competition between underwriters.
    d. Applies to debt issues only.
    e. None of the above.

7. Which of the following statements describe(s) shelf registration?
    a. Reduces competition between underwriters.
    b. Eliminates the underpricing problem.
    c. Applies to equity issues only.
*   d. Allows a number of issues to be made under the same registration statement.
    e. None of the above.

8. The price of a stock tends to decline when the company issues additional shares because:
    a. Increased supply, with a constant demand, implies a drop in price.
    b. The market anticipates that managers will issue stock when they think the stock is undervalued.
    c. Book value per share decreases.
*   d. The market anticipates that managers will issue stock when they think the stock is overvalued.
    e. None of the above.

9. The advertisement of a public issue that lists all the underwriters is known as the:
    a. Red herring.
    b. Prospectus.
*   c. Tombstone.
    d. Tear sheet.
    e. None of the above.

10. The advantages of a private debt placement (relative to a corresponding public placement) include:
    a. Lower issue costs.
    b. More flexible loan arrangements.
    c. No SEC registration is required.
    d. Easier renegotiation of terms, if necessary.
*   e. All of the above.

115

11. Which of the following statements characterizes private placements of debt:
   a. Must be registered with the SEC if over $100 million.
   * b. Must be sold to a small group of knowledgeable investors.
   c. Issue costs are higher than for public issues.
   d. Covenants are usually tighter and harder to modify than for public issues.
   e. Rarely used by large, publicly traded firms.

12. Privately placed debt typically requires a yield that is:
   a. The same as the yield on a similar public offering.
   b. About 50 basis points below that on a similar public offering.
   * c. About 50 basis points above that on a similar public offering.
   d. Directly related to the dividend yield on the company's common stock.
   e. None of the above.

13. The top underwriter for the first half of 1995 was:
   a. CS First Boston.
   b. Goldman Sachs.
   c. First Tennessee.
   d. Lehman Brothers.
   * e. None of the above.

14. When a company has a rights issue, it is common for an underwriter to agree to purchase all unsubscribed stock. The fee for performing this service is the:
   * a. Standby fee.
   b. Preemptive right.
   c. Take-up fee.
   d. Registration fee.
   e. None of the above.

15. The Upas Drug Company is making a rights issue at $8 a share of one new share for every five shares currently held. If the stock price before the issue was $20, what is the likely ex-rights price?
   a. $ 8
   b. $16
   * c. $18
   d. $20
   e. None of the above.

16. The Upas Drug Company is making a rights issue at $8 a share of one new share for every five shares currently held, and the stock price before the issue was $20.
   Suppose Upas had set the issue price at $12 a share. If the company still wished to raise the same amount of money, how would the rest of the issue terms have to change?
*   a. Two new shares for every 15 held.
     b. Two new shares for every 10 held.
     c. One new share for every 8 held.
     d. None of the above.

17. Circe Hams is making a rights issue at $5 a share of one new share for every two shares currently held. The stock price before the issue was $20. Suppose that you currently own 2,000 shares and that you wish to maintain the same dollar stake in the company after the issue. How many rights should you sell?
*   a. 333
     b. 667
     c. 1,000
     d. 2,000
     e. None.

18. The Miller Drug Company is making a rights issue at $10 a share of one new share for every ten shares currently held. If the stock price before the issue was $40, what is the likely ex-rights price?
     a. $10.00
     b. $40.00
*   c. $37.27
     d. $41.00
     e. None of the above.

19 The Wilson Company is making a rights issue at $4 a share of one new share for every three shares currently held. If the stock price before the issue was $50, what is the likely ex-rights price?
     a. $ 4.00
*   b. $38.50
     c. $51.33
     d. $50.00
     e. None of the above.

20. Waldo & Company is making a rights issue at $15 a share of one new share for every two shares currently held. If the stock price before the issue was $30, what is the likely ex-rights price?
    a. $15
    b. $30
    c. $18.75
    d. $26.33
*   e. None of the above.

Chapter 15 - True-False Questions

T 1. Recently, most venture capital money has come from pension funds.

F 2. Venture capital partnerships generally put up the full amount of cash required to take a startup company to successful introduction of its product. However, the venture capitalists will demand a majority of equity shares and control of the startup company's board of directors.

T 3. Venture capital funding is typically raised in stages. A successful startup may go through several rounds of financing before going public in an initial public offering.

F 5. The preliminary prospectus is known as a "tombstone."

T 6. Most public issues must be registered with the SEC, and the company may not sell securities until its registration statement has been approved by the SEC.

F 7. Underpricing is not a serious problem for most Initial Public Offerings (IPOs).

T 8. Details of a public issue together with information about the company are contained in the issue prospectus.

F 9. The duties of the transfer agent include preventing any unauthorized issue of securities.

T 10. In the issuance of common stock, underwriters play a triple role - they provide advice to the company, buy the issue, and resell it to the public.

F 11. Any issue of stock must be approved by the firm's stockholders.

T 12. In a cash offer, underwriters receive a spread, which is equal to the difference between the price that they pay for the issue and the price at which they resell it.

F 13. A public issue can be offered either to investors at large or directly to existing shareholders. The first method is called a privileged subscription issue; the second is called a rights issue.

T 14. Shelf registration allows the firm to file a registration statement with the SEC to cover a series of subsequent stock or debt issues.

F   15.   Underwriting spreads are independent of the size of the issue.

T   16.   The underwriting spread for debt is generally less than that for equity.

F   17.   Managers are more likely to issue stock when they think the stock is undervalued.

T   18.   A large part of the cost of issuing securities is fixed.

F   19.   It is less expensive to issue stock than to issue the same amount of debt.

T   20.   Privately placed common stock is known as "letter" stock.

F   21.   The first public issue by a company is known as a seasoned issue.

T   22.   Announcing a new stock issue generally depresses stock price. Investors seem to regard the decision to issue as a negative signal about firm value.

F   23.   When companies make their first public issue of stock, the offer price is generally pitched above the subsequent market price.

T   24.   In a rights offer, underwriters may receive a standby fee and a take-up fee.

F   25.   Issuing stock below book value per share reduces earnings per share and stockholders' wealth.

T   26.   The difference between the rights-on price and the ex-rights price represents the value of the right.

F   27.   Virtually all debt is sold by a rights offer. Equity securities may or may not be sold by a rights offer.

T   28.   The issue price is largely irrelevant in a rights offering as long as the rights are exercised.

F   29.   In general, the stock price is the same before as after a rights issue.

T   30.   Rights issues are generally cheaper than cash offers, and yet many corporations avoid rights issues.

Chapter 15 - Essay Questions

1. Discuss the advantages of shelf registration.

Answer

Shelf registration, allowed under SEC Rule 415, conveys several advantages to companies issuing securities, whether debt or equity:
- Securities can be issued in bits and pieces, without incurring excessive transactions costs.
- Securities can be issued on short notice.
- Securities can be issued so as to take advantage of favorable market conditions.
- The issuing firm can require underwriters to compete for its business.

2. Discuss the role of the underwriter.

Answer

The underwriter is a very necessary part of the securities market. Most firms do not issue securities very often and so must go outside the firm for the expertise necessary to cope with the current laws and regulations that affect such issues. In addition, underwriters are very close to the market and hence have the expertise and contacts necessary to both design and distribute the securities. Thus, underwriters have a triple role: They provide advice and guidance in the preparation of the security issue, they price it, and they sell it.

Chapter 16 - Multiple Choice Questions

1. Which of the following dividends is/are never in the form of cash?
   a. Regular dividend.
   * b. Stock dividend.
   c. Extra dividend.
   d. Liquidating dividend.
   e. None of the above.

2. Which of these dates is last in time?
   * a. Payment date.
   b. With-dividend date.
   c. Dividend declaration date.
   d. Ex-dividend date.
   e. Record date.

3. In economic terms, share repurchase is most similar to:
   a. A stock split.
   b. Greenmail.
   c. Payment of a stock dividend.
   d. A reverse stock split.
   * e. Payment of a cash dividend.

4. Greenmail refers to the practice of a company purchasing its stock from:
   a. Small shareholders who are unhappy with company performance.
   b. Large shareholders who are unhappy with company performance.
   * c. A hostile shareholder who threatens to take over the firm.
   d. All shareholders.
   e. None of the above.

5. Which of the following is not true?
   a. Firms have long-run target dividend payout ratios.
   b. Managers focus more on dividend changes than on absolute levels.
   c. Dividend changes follow shifts in long-run, sustainable earnings.
   d. Managers are reluctant to make dividend changes that might have to be reversed.
   * e. None of the above.

6. What is the Lintner model of dividends?
   a. $DIV_1 - DIV_0$ = target ratio (adjustment rate·DIV_0 - EPS_1)
   b. $DIV_1 - DIV_0$ = adjustment rate (target ratio·DIV_0 - EPS_1)
 * c. $DIV_1 - DIV_0$ = adjustment rate (target ratio·EPS_1 - DIV_0)
   d. DIV_1 = adjustment rate (target ratio·EPS_1 - DIV_0)
   e. None of the above.

7. One key assumption of the Miller and Modigliani dividend irrelevance argument is that:
   a. Future stock prices are certain.
   b. There are no capital gains taxes.
   c. All investments are risk-free.
 * d. New shares are sold at a fair price.

8. One possible reason that shareholders often insist on higher dividends is:
   a. They agree with Miller and Modigliani.
 * b. They do not trust managers to spend retained earnings wisely.
   c. The stock market is efficient.
   d. Tax considerations.
   e. None of the above.

9. If investors do not like dividends because of the extra taxes that they require, how would you expect the stock price to behave on the ex-dividend date?
   a. Fall by more than the amount of the dividend.
   b. Fall by the amount of the dividend.
 * c. Fall by less than the amount of the dividend.

10. If dividends are taxed more heavily than capital gains, then investors:
 * a. Should pay more for stocks with low dividend yields.
   b. Should pay more for stocks with high dividend yields.
   c. Should pay the same for stocks with high or low dividend yields.

11. If dividends are taxed more heavily than capital gains, then investors:
   a. Should accept a lower pretax rate of return from stocks with high dividend yields.
 * b. Should accept a lower pretax rate of return from stocks with low dividend yields.
   c. Should require the same pretax rate of return from stocks with high or low dividend yields.

12. The leftist position is that the market will reward firms that:
    a. Have a high dividend yield.
    * b. Have a low dividend yield.
    c. Are well managed, regardless of dividend yield.
    d. None of the above.

13. The rightist position is that the market will reward firms that:
    * a. Have a high dividend yield.
    b. Have a low dividend yield.
    c. Are well managed, regardless of dividend yield.
    d. None of the above.

14. Which of the following investors has/have the strongest tax reason to prefer dividends over capital gains?
    a. Pension funds.
    b. Private individuals.
    c. Insurance companies.
    * d. Corporations.

15. A firm has $1 per share in cash, which it will use either to repurchase shares or to pay a cash dividend. Share price is $20. Other things equal, the share price after a repurchase will be:
    * a. $20
    b. $21
    c. $19
    d. $18
    e. None of the above.

16. A firm has $2 per share in cash, which it will use either to repurchase shares or to pay a cash dividend. Share price is $30. Other things equal, the share price after a repurchase will be:
    a. $28
    b. $32
    * c. $30
    d. $26
    e. None of the above.

17. What is the effective tax rate on dividends received by a corporation?
    a. 35.0 percent.
    b. 30.0 percent.
    c. 20.0 percent.
    * d. 10.5 percent.

18. You own 500 shares of Tar Heel Shoe, selling at $35 per share and paying an annual dividend of $2 per share. You depend on the dividend to pay the rent. Suppose the firm eliminates the dividend and repurchases shares instead. What will you be able to do to replace next year's dividend check?
* a. Sell 28.6 shares at $35.
  b. Sell 27.0 shares at $37.
  c. Sell 30.3 shares at $33.
  d. Sell 500 shares at $2.

19. You own 100 shares of BarTop Inc., selling at $75 per share and paying an annual dividend of $5 per share. You depend on the dividend to buy books. Suppose the firm eliminates the dividend and repurchases shares instead. What will you be able to do to replace next year's dividend check?
  a. Sell 7.1 shares at $70.
  b. Sell 6.3 shares at $80.
  c. Sell 100 shares at $5.
* d. Sell 6.7 shares at $75.

20. With respect to the taxation of dividends, the United States has:
  a. A single-rate system.
  b. A split-rate system.
* c. A two-tier system.
  d. An imputation system.
  e. None of the above.

21. Under which system of taxation might a shareholder receive a refund from the government for corporate taxes paid?
  a. A single-rate system.
  b. A split-rate system.
  c. A two-tier system.
* d. An imputation system.
  e. None of the above.

Chapter 16 - True-False Questions

F 1. A stock dividend is very similar to a stock split except that stock dividends cannot exceed 5 percent of previously outstanding shares.

T 2. An alternative to paying cash dividends is to repurchase stock.

F 3. State law forbids companies from paying dividends out of surplus.

T 4. If a dividend is unlikely to be repeated in the future, it is usually called a "special" dividend.

F 5. Dividends are sent to all shareholders who are registered on the ex-dividend date.

T 6. Cash dividends are taxed as ordinary income.

F 7. Because greenmail involves the repurchase of stock at a price higher than the market price, all shareholders benefit.

T 8. Firms have long-run target dividend payout ratios.

F 9. Mature companies with stable earnings usually pay out a low proportion of earnings.

T 10. Managers are reluctant to make dividend changes that might have to be reversed.

F 11. Dividend changes precede shifts in long-run, sustainable earnings.

T 12. This year's dividend payment depends on this year's earnings as well as last year's earnings.

F 13. The evidence suggests that when companies pay lower dividends than is suggested by past earnings, subsequent earnings usually increase.

T 14. Dividends anticipate future earnings.

F 15. The Miller and Modigliani argument for the irrelevance of dividend policy assumes a world of certainty and efficient markets.

T 16. If a firm fixes its investment and borrowing policy, additional cash dividends can come only from the sale of shares.

F   17. Miller and Modigliani argue that investors prefer a company with a high-dividend payout.

T   18. Miller and Modigliani's argument for dividend irrelevance assumes an efficient market.

F   19. Because a dividend received is "cash in hand" and a capital gain is only a "paper gain," investors prefer a company with a high-dividend payout.

T   20. If dividends are taxed more heavily than capital gains, investors should pay more for stocks with low-dividend yields.

F   21. Other things equal, a high tax rate on dividends means that investors expect a lower rate of return on high-payout stocks.

T   22. Shareholders whose stock has been repurchased are subject to tax on any capital gains realized by the sale.

F   23. Miller and Modigliani point out that, because dividends are more predictable than capital gains, a low-payout policy can increase company risk, but they argue that this is exactly offset by the increased return.

T   24. Corporations pay corporate income tax on only 30 percent of dividends received.

F   25. Most empirical studies support the view that investors require a higher rate of return on low-dividend stocks.

T   26. The Tax Reform Act of 1986 reduced the tax advantages of investing in low-payout companies.

Chapter 16 - Essay Questions

1. The rightists argue that increasing a firm's dividend will increase the value of the company. Defend this position.

Answer
The key arguments made by rightists are:
- Investors prefer cash dividends to "paper" capital gains.
- Investors do not trust managers to invest retained earnings wisely.
- Many investors need the cash from dividends for living expenses, for example, those who are retired; this clientele prefers high dividends.
- Many investors mistrust the information made public by companies and so rely on cash dividends to judge corporate success.

2. The leftists argue that decreasing a firm's dividend will increase the value of the company. Defend this position.

Answer
The main argument made by leftists is that low dividends reduce the tax burden on shareholders, because the effective tax rate on capital gains is less than the tax rate on dividends.

3. Discuss three different ways different countries tax dividends.

Answer
Three different countries and their dividend taxation schemes are:
- The United States. This is a *two-tier scheme*, where corporate profits are taxed and dividends paid out of after-tax corporate profits; these dividends are also taxed at the personal level.
- Germany. This is a *split-rate scheme*, where profits that are retained by a corporation are taxed at a higher rate than are profits that are distributed as dividends.
- Australia. This is an *imputation scheme*, where shareholders are taxed on dividends, but shareholders may deduct from their tax bill their share of the corporate tax that was paid by the company.

Chapter 17 - Multiple Choice Questions

1. Under what conditions would a policy of maximizing the value of the firm not be the same as a policy of maximizing shareholder wealth?
    a. If issuing debt increases the probability of bankruptcy.
    b. If the firm issues debt for the first time.
* c. If an issue of debt affects the value of existing debt.
    d. If the beta of the equity is positive.

2. The law of conservation of value implies that:
* a. The value of any asset is preserved regardless of the nature of the claims against it.
    b. The value of a firm's common stock is unchanged when debt is added to its capital structure.
    c. The value of a firm's debt is unchanged when common stock is added to its capital structure.
    d. None of the above.

3. Miller and Modigliani's Proposition I states that:
    a. The market value of a firm's common stock is independent of its capital structure.
    b. The market value of a firm's debt is independent of its capital structure.
    c. A and B.
* d. The market value of any firm is independent of its capital structure.
    e. None of the above.

4. Doyce & Clennam is financed entirely by common stock which is priced to offer a 15 percent expected return. If the company repurchases 25 percent of the common stock and substitutes an equal value of debt yielding 6 percent, what is the expected return on the common stock after the refinancing?
    a. 22 percent.
* b. 18 percent.
    c. 16 percent.
    d. 12.75 percent.
    e. None of the above.

5. Look again at question 4. Suppose that before the refinancing, the stock price is $40 and that earnings per share are expected to be $6. What are expected earnings per share after the refinancing?
    a. $6.00
* b. $7.20
    c. $7.50
    d. None of the above.

6. Look one more time at questions 4 and 5. Suppose that before the refinancing, an investor held 12 shares of Doyce & Clennam stock. What should she do if she wishes to ensure that the risk and expected return on her investment are unaffected by the refinancing?
      a. Continue to hold 12 shares.
*   b. Sell 3 shares and buy $120 of debt.
      c. Borrow $120 and buy a further 3 shares.
      d. This is impossible; there is no way to keep the risk and expected return the same.

7. Doyle & Co. is financed entirely by common stock which is priced to offer a 20 percent expected return. If the company repurchases 40 percent of the common stock and substitutes an equal value of debt yielding 8 percent, what is the expected return on the common stock after the refinancing?
      a. 16 percent.
      b. 20 percent.
      c. 25 percent.
*   d. 28 percent.
      e. None of the above.

8. Look again at question 7. Suppose that before the refinancing, the stock price is $60 and that earnings per share are expected to be $12. What are expected earnings per share after the refinancing?
      a. $12.00
      b. $15.00
*   c. $16.80
      d. $18.00
      e. None of the above.

9. Look one more time at questions 7 and 8. Suppose that before the refinancing, an investor held 100 shares of common stock. What should he do if he wishes to ensure that the risk and expected return on his investment are unaffected by the refinancing?
*   a. Sell 40 shares and buy $2,400 of debt.
      b. Continue to hold 100 shares.
      c. Borrow $2,400 and buy a further 40 shares.
      d. This is impossible; there is no way to keep the risk and expected return the same.

10. D&S Co. is financed entirely by common stock which is priced to offer a 27 percent expected return. If the company repurchases 10 percent of the common stock and substitutes an equal value of debt yielding 7 percent, what is the expected return on the common stock after the refinancing?
   a. 20.7 percent.
* b. 29.2 percent.
   c. 27.0 percent.
   d. 30.0 percent.
   e. None of the above.

11. Look again at question 10. Suppose that before the refinancing, the stock price is $80 and that earnings per share are expected to be $21.60. What are expected earnings per share after the refinancing?
   a. $21.60
   b. $23.76
   c. $25.00
* d. $23.36
   e. None of the above.

12. Look one more time at questions 10 and 11. Suppose that before the refinancing, an investor held 200 shares of common stock. What should she do if she wishes to ensure that the risk and expected return on her investment are unaffected by the refinancing?
   a. Borrow $1,600 and buy a further 20 shares.
   b. Continue to hold 200 shares.
* c. Sell 20 shares and buy $1,600 of debt.
   d. This is impossible; there is no way to keep the risk and expected return the same.

13. According to Miller and Modigliani's Proposition II:
   a. The debtholders' expected rate of return will increase as the firm's debt-equity ratio increases.
   b. The shareholders' expected rate of return is independent of the firm's debt-equity ratio.
   c. The debtholders' expected rate of return is independent of the firm's debt-equity ratio.
* d. The shareholders' expected rate of return will increase as the firm's debt-equity ratio increases.
   e. None of the above.

14. Suppose that a firm is financed with 70% equity and 30% debt and that the interest rate on the debt is 8 percent and the expected return on the common stock is 17 percent. What is the firm's weighted average cost of capital?
    a. 10.70 percent.
    b. 12.50 percent.
*   c. 14.30 percent.
    d. 17.00 percent.
    e. None of the above.

15. Suppose that a firm is financed with 80% equity and 20% debt and that the interest rate on the debt is 6 percent and the expected return on the common stock is 16 percent. What is the firm's weighted average cost of capital?
    a. 8.00 percent.
    b. 12.00 percent.
    c. 16.00 percent.
    d. 18.00 percent.
*   e. None of the above.

16. The Vulcan Forge Company is financed entirely by common stock, which has a beta of .7 and a total market value of $80 million. Suppose the firm repurchases $30 million of stock and replaces it with risk-free debt. What is the beta of the stock after the refinancing?
*   a. 1.12
    b. 1.19
    c. .56
    d. .44
    e. None of the above.

17. The Valley Company is financed entirely by common stock which has a beta of 1.6 and a total market value of $150 million. Suppose the firm repurchases $30 million of stock and replaces it with risk-free debt. What is the beta of the stock after the refinancing?
    a. .48
    b. 1.20
    c. 1.60
*   d. 2.00
    e. None of the above.

18. The V&L Company is financed entirely by common stock which has a beta of 1.8 and a total market value of $200 million. Suppose the firm repurchases $50 million of stock and replaces it with risk-free debt. What is the beta of the stock after the refinancing?
    a. 2.60
    b. 2.20
    c. 2.00
    d. 1.80
*   e. None of the above.

19. The "traditional" view of capital structure is that the weighted average cost of capital:
*   a. Falls with moderate levels of leverage and then increases.
    b. Does not change with leverage.
    c. Increases with moderate levels of leverage and then falls.
    d. Increases as leverage increases.

20. The traditionalist view of capital structure and the Miller and Modigliani view are different because:
    a. Miller and Modigliani assume risk-free debt.
    b. The traditionalists assume risk-free debt.
    c. Miller and Modigliani ignore the increase in stockholder risk as the debt-equity ratio increases.
*   d. The traditionalists ignore the increase in stockholder risk as the debt-equity ratio increases.

Chapter 17 - True-False Questions

T   1. Whenever a firm goes into debt, it is creating financial leverage.

F   2. Proposition I states that the value of the firm is determined by the proportions of debt and equity securities that are issued.

T   3. Financial leverage increases the expected return and risk of the shareholder.

F   4. Proposition I assumes that debt is risk free.

T   5. The choice of capital structure is essentially a marketing problem.

F   6. Proposition I implies that leverage increases earnings per share but leaves the price-earnings multiple unchanged.

T   7. Proposition I implies that financial leverage has no effect on firm value.

F   8. In perfect capital markets, the company's capital structure does not affect either its operating income or its total market value, but it does affect the expected return on the firm's assets.

T   9. Financial leverage increases the expected stream of earnings per share but does not change the share price.

F   10. The expected return on assets depends on several factors including the firm's capital structure.

T   11. The weighted average cost of capital is the expected return on a portfolio of all the firm's securities.

F   12. According to Proposition II, the rate of return required by the debtholders increases as the firm's debt-equity ratio increases.

T   13. Proposition II states that the rate of return that shareholders require increases as the firm's debt-equity ratio increases.

F   14. The expected rate of return on equity is independent of capital structure so long as the probability of default is zero.

T   15. Under Proposition II the cost of equity increases as more debt is issued, but the weighted average cost of capital remains unchanged.

F   16. Since the expected rate of return on debt is less than the expected rate of return on equity, the weighted average cost of capital declines as more debt is issued.

T   17. The beta of the firm is equal to the weighted average of the betas on its debt and equity.

F   18. The traditional view of debt policy argues that moderate amounts of leverage increase the expected equity return, but that expected equity return declines when the firm borrows too much. The optimal capital structure is the point at which the expected equity return is at a maximum.

T   19. The traditional view of debt policy argues that moderate amounts of leverage increase the expected equity return, but that expected equity return declines when the firm borrows too much. The optimal capital structure is the point at which the weighted average cost of capital is a minimum.

F   20. The capital structure that maximizes the value of the firm also minimizes the weighted average cost of capital.

Chapter 17 - Essay Questions

1. Discuss the traditional position on capital structure.

Answer
   The traditional view of debt policy argues that moderate amounts of leverage increase the expected equity return, but that expected equity return declines when the firm borrows too much. The optimal capital structure is the point at which the weighted average cost of capital is a minimum. The difficulty with this position is that it:
   -Assumes the goal is to minimize company cost of capital instead of maximizing value.
   -Ignores the fact that, as the debt-equity ratio increases, the stockholders will demand a higher rate of return.

The traditional position might make sense if the corporation could borrow more cheaply than individual investors, but this seems unlikely in practice; mortgage rates, for example, are usually quite close to long-term corporate bond rates.

2. Discuss examples of financial managers' attempts to add value to their corporations through financing.

Answer
   The key to adding value through financing is to find a clientele with an unsatisfied need and to meet this need quickly, before financial markets evolve to the point where the opportunity is lost. Examples include:
   -Pfizer's unbundled stock units (USUs), which failed.
   -General Motors' preferred equity redemption cumulative stock (PERCS), which satisfied a limited demand.
   -Citicorp's floating-rate notes, which were quite successful.

Chapter 18 - Multiple Choice Questions

1. If a firm permanently borrows $25 million at an interest rate of 8 percent, what is the present value of the interest tax shield? Assume a 35 percent tax rate.
   a. $8.00 million.
 * b. $8.75 million.
   c. $16.50 million.
   d. $25.00 million.
   e.   None of the above.

2. If a firm borrows $25 million for one year at an interest rate of 8 percent, what is the present value of the interest tax shield? Assume a 35 percent tax rate.
 * a. $648,000
   b. $700,000
   c. $1,000,000
   d. $25,000,000
   e.   None of the above.

3. If a firm permanently borrows $50 million at an interest rate of 9 percent, what is the present value of the interest tax shield? Assume a 35 percent tax rate.
   a. $50.00 million.
   b. $25.00 million.
 * c. $17.50 million.
   d. $ 8.75 million.
   e.   None of the above.

4. If a firm borrows $50 million for one year at an interest rate of 9 percent, what is the present value of the interest tax shield? Assume a 35 percent tax rate.
   a. $50.00 million.
   b. $17.50 million.
   c. $1.58 million.
 * d. $ 1.44 million.
   e.   None of the above.

5. Dombey and Son's balance sheet is as follows (NWC = net working capital; LTA = long-term assets; D = debt; E = equity; V = firm value):

	Book Values				Market Values		
NWC	200	500	D	NWC	200	500	D
LTA	2300	2000	E	LTA	2800	2500	E
	2500	2500	V		3000	3000	V

According to MM's Proposition I corrected for taxes, what will be the change in company value if Dombey issues $200 of equity and uses it to make a permanent reduction in the company's debt? Assume a 35 percent tax rate.
   a. $140
   b. $70
   c. $0
* d. -$70
   e. -$140

6. The relative tax advantage of debt is:
   a.
   $$\frac{1 - T_c}{(1 - T_{pE})(1 - T_c)}$$

* b.
   $$\frac{1 - T_p}{(1 - T_{pE})(1 - T_c)}$$

   c.
   $$\frac{1 - T_p}{(1 - T_p)(1 - T_c)}$$

   d.
   $$\frac{1 - T_p}{(1 - T_{pE})(1 + T_c)}$$

   e. None of the above.

7. Suppose that a company can direct $1 to either debt interest or capital gains for equity investors. If there were no personal taxes on capital gains, which of the following investors would not care how the money was channeled? The corporate tax rate is 35%.
    a. Investors paying zero personal tax.
    b. Investors paying personal tax of 17 percent.
*   c. Investors paying personal tax of 35 percent.
    d. Investors paying personal tax of 52 percent.
    e. None of the above.

8. Look again at question 7. Suppose that half of equity income were subject to personal tax (e.g., half is taxable dividends and half is tax-free capital gains). Which investors now would not care how the money was channelled?
    a. Investors paying zero personal tax.
    b. Investors paying personal tax of 17 percent.
    c. Investors paying personal tax of 35 percent.
*   d. Investors paying personal tax of 52 percent.
    e. None of the above.

9. Suppose that the expected return on a safe, zero-NPV, all-equity-financed project is 8 percent. What, according to Miller, is the interest rate on risk-free debt? Assume a 35 percent corporate tax rate.
    a. 5.20 percent.
    b. 8.00 percent.
*   c. 12.30 percent.
    d. 17.39 percent.
    e. None of the above.

10. Suppose that the expected return on a safe, zero-NPV, all-equity-financed project is 10 percent. What, according to Miller, is the interest rate on risk-free debt? Assume a 35 percent corporate tax rate.
    a. 6.50 percent.
    b. 8.00 percent.
    c. 10.00 percent.
    d. 28.57 percent.
*   e. None of the above.

11. If Miller is right and AAA corporate bonds yield 15 percent, what should be the yield on AAA municipal bonds? Assume a 35 percent corporate tax rate.
* a. 9.75 percent.
  b. 12.35 percent.
  c. 15.00 percent.
  d. 23.08 percent.
  e. None of the above.

12. If companies are unsure whether they will make taxable profits in the future:
* a. Safe, profitable companies will have an incentive to issue more debt than risky, unprofitable companies.
  b. The aggregate amount of debt issued will be higher than predicted by Miller's theory of debt and taxes.
  c. The equilibrium interest rate on corporate debt will be higher than predicted by Miller.
  d. None of the above.

13. What are some of the possible consequences of financial distress?
  a. Debtholders, who face the prospect of getting only part of their money back, are likely to want the company to take additional risks.
* b. Debtholders would like equity holders to put up more money, even if it is invested in zero-NPV projects.
  c. Equity investors would like the company to cut its dividend payments to conserve cash.
  d. Equity investors would like the firm to shift toward less risky lines of business.
  e. None of the above.

14. What are some of the possible consequences of financial distress?
  a. Debtholders, who face the prospect of getting only part of their money back, are likely to want the company to take additional risks.
  b. Equity investors would like the company to cut its dividend payments to conserve cash.
* c. Equity investors would like the firm to shift toward riskier lines of business.
  d. Equity investors would like the firm to settle up with creditors as fast as possible.

15. The trade-off theory of capital structure predicts that:
    a. Unprofitable firms should borrow more then profitable ones.
    * b. Safe firms should borrow more than risky ones.
    c. Rapidly growing firms should borrow more than mature firms.
    d. Increasing leverage increases firm value.
    e. D and C.

16. The trade-off theory of capital structure predicts that:
    a. Unprofitable firms should borrow more then profitable ones.
    b. Safe firms should borrow less than risky ones.
    c. Rapidly growing firms should borrow more than mature firms.
    d. Increasing leverage increases firm value.
    * e. Unprofitable companies with risky, intangible assets ought to rely primarily on equity financing.

17. The pecking order theory of capital structure predicts that:
    * a. If two firms are equally profitable, the more rapidly growing firm will borrow more, other things equal.
    b. Firms prefer equity to debt financing.
    c. Risky firms will end up borrowing less.
    d. Risky firms will end up borrowing more.

18. The pecking order theory of capital structure predicts that:
    a. Risky firms will end up borrowing less.
    b. Firms prefer equity to debt financing.
    * c. Firms prefer debt to equity when external financing is required.
    d. Risky firms will end up borrowing more.

19. Financial slack means:
    a. Cash and marketable securities.
    b. Readily saleable real assets.
    c. Ready access to the debt markets.
    d. Ready access to the equity markets.
    * e. All of the above.

20. The pecking order theory of capital structure is based on:
    a. The risk of company assets.
    b. The growth of company assets.
    c. The issue costs of debt versus equity.
    * d. Asymmetric information.

Chapter 18 - True-False Questions

F   1. The present value of the interest tax shield is the same regardless of whether a firm plans to borrow permanently or temporarily.

T   2. Usually we discount the interest tax shield at the rate of interest on the firm's debt.

F   3. MM's Proposition I corrected for corporate taxes states that:
Value of firm = Value if all-equity-financed - PV tax shield

T   4. MM's Proposition I corrected for corporate taxes implies that an issue of permanent debt increases shareholders' wealth by the value of the debt times the corporate tax rate.

F   5. Miller's model implies that investors whose marginal rate of tax on income exceeds the corporate tax rate will prefer to hold bonds. The remainder will prefer to hold equity.

T   6. The tax incentives to issue debt are highest for profitable companies which are sure to pay taxes in the future.

F   7. Miller's model implies that, risk apart, the rate of interest on a firm's debt is equal to the expected return on its equity grossed up at the rate of corporate income tax.

T   8. The relative tax advantage of debt is:

$$\frac{1 - T_p}{(1 - T_{pE})(1 - T_c)}$$

F   9. Investors should be willing to hold corporate bonds only if the pre-tax yield on them is at least as high as the after-tax yield on municipals.

T   10. The corporate tax shield on interest payments is worth more to some firms than to others.

F   11. Interest on municipal bonds is not taxed; therefore municipals offer higher pre-tax yields.

T   12. Bankruptcy is a legal mechanism that allows creditors to take over when the firm defaults.

F   13. When a firm is in financial distress, an increase in business risk reduces share value.

T 14. Because creditors foresee the costs of bankruptcy, they charge a higher rate of interest to compensate for the present value of these costs.

F 15. It is always in the interests of shareholders to provide money for positive-NPV projects.

T 16. What little evidence there is suggests that the present value of expected bankruptcy costs is generally small.

F 17. When a firm is in financial distress, a dividend payment reduces share value by more than the amount of the dividend because it takes valuable resources away from the firm.

T 18. Costs of financial distress are likely to be highest for firms with valuable intangible assets and growth opportunities.

F 19. It is better for firms with large accumulated losses to borrow than it is for firms that are tax-paying.

T 20. According to the trade-off theory, more profitable firms should have more debt and thus the highest debt ratios.

F 21. In practice, the more profitable firms have the highest debt capacity and the highest debt ratios.

T 22. The trade-off theory states that companies with safe, tangible assets and plenty of taxable income ought to have high debt ratios.

F 23. The pecking order theory of capital structure does not distinguish between internally generated equity funds (i.e., retained earnings) and externally generated equity funds (i.e., funds raised through a stock issue).

T 24. The pecking order theory implies that firms prefer internal to external financing.

Chapter 18 - Essay Questions

1. Discuss the basic idea behind Miller's arguments about debt and taxes.

Answer
The basic idea is that, in equilibrium, taxes determine the aggregate amount of corporate debt but not the amount issued by any particular firm. That is, given tax rates, the market will adjust until there is no advantage to any company issuing more (or less) debt than it currently has outstanding.

2. Discuss some examples of the conflicts that may arise between debtholders and stockholders when a company encounters financial distress.

Answer
These conflicts occur because, when a firm is in financial distress, the shareholders' goal of increasing the value of the common stock may result in actions that decrease the value of the company, thus hurting the debtholders. Some examples of such activities are risk shifting, refusing to contribute equity capital, cash-in-and-run, and playing for time.

3. Explain the pecking order theory of capital structure.

Answer
This theory is based on the observation that, in general, managers know more about their company's prospects than do outsiders. Thus, there will be a tendency for managers to issue stock when they feel their stock is overpriced, and to issue debt when they think their stock is underpriced. Thus, to the capital markets, all else equal, an issue of debt is good news and an issue of stock is bad news.

Chapter 19 - Multiple Choice Questions

1. Which of the following statements characterize(s) the weighted average cost of capital formula?
* a. It requires knowledge of the required return on equity.
  b. It requires knowledge of the required return on the firm if it is all-equity financed.
  c. It is based on book values of debt and equity.
  d. It can be used to take account of issue costs and other such financing side effects.
  e. None of the above.

2. Which of the following statements characterize(s) the weighted average cost of capital formula?
  a. It requires knowledge of the required return on the firm if it is all-equity financed.
  b. It is based on book values of debt and equity.
* c. It assumes the project is a carbon copy of the firm.
  d. It can be used to take account of issue costs and other such financing side effects.
  e. None of the above.

3. A firm is financed with 30% risk-free debt and 70% equity. The risk-free rate is 8%, the firm's cost of equity capital is 15%, and the firm's marginal tax rate is 35%. What is the firm's weighted average cost of capital?
  a. 8.00%
* b. 12.06%
  c. 15.00%
  d. 21.43%
  e. None of the above.

4. A firm is financed with 40% risk-free debt and 60% equity. The risk-free rate is 7%, the firm's cost of equity capital is 18%, and the firm's marginal tax rate is 35%. What is the firm's weighted average cost of capital?
  a. 18.00%
  b. 7.00%
  c. 13.60%
* d. 12.62%
  e. None of the above.

5. A firm is financed with 25% risk-free debt and 75% equity. The risk-free rate is 6%, the firm's cost of equity capital is 25%, and the firm's marginal tax rate is 35%. What is the firm's weighted average cost of capital?
    a. 20.25%
    b. 6.00%
    c. 25.00%
    d. 17.56%
*   e. None of the above.

6. A project costs $15 million and is expected to produce cash flows of $3 million a year for 10 years. The opportunity cost of capital is 14%. If the firm has to issue stock to undertake the project and issue costs are $500,000, what is the project's APV?
    a. -$352,000
*   b. $148,000
    c. $648,000
    d. $952,000
    e. None of the above.

7. A project costs $14 million and is expected to produce cash flows of $4 million a year for 15 years. The opportunity cost of capital is 20%. If the firm has to issue stock to undertake the project and issue costs are $1 million, what is the project's APV?
*   a. $3.7 million
    b. $4.5 million
    c. $4.7 million
    d. $3.0 million
    e. None of the above.

8. A project costs $7 million and is expected to produce cash flows of $2 million a year for 10 years. The opportunity cost of capital is 16%. If the firm has to issue stock to undertake the project and issue costs are $.5 million, what is the project's APV?
    a. $9.67 million
    b. $2.67 million
    c. $1.67 million
    d. $0.67 million
*   e. None of the above.

9. A project will generate a forecasted interest tax shield of $150,000 per year in perpetuity. If the firm's borrowing rate is 7% and the opportunity cost of capital is 16%, what is the present value of the tax shield? Assume debt is rebalanced each year (rule 2).
   a. $ 937,500
   b. $1,087,500
* c. $1,016,355
   d. $2,142,857
   e. None of the above.

10. A project will generate a forecasted interest tax shield of $10,000 per year in perpetuity. If the firm's borrowing rate is 9% and the opportunity cost of capital is 25%, what is the present value of the tax shield? Assume debt is rebalanced each year (rule 2).
   a. $50,000
* b. $45,872
   c. $36,698
   d. $40,000
   e. None of the above.

11. The Miles-Ezzell formula for the adjusted cost of capital assumes that:
* a. Debt capacity is a constant proportion of project value.
   b. The project is a perpetuity.
   c. The project is a carbon copy of the firm.
   d. MM's Proposition I corrected for taxes holds (i.e., $T^* = T_c = .35$).
   e. All of the above.

12. The MM formula for the adjusted cost of capital assumes that:
   a. Debt capacity is a constant proportion of project value.
   b. The project is a perpetuity.
   c. The project is a carbon copy of the firm.
   d. Debt capacity is fixed and permanent.
* e. B and D.

13. A project costs $100 million, offers a perpetual cash flow stream, and adds $30 million to the firm's debt capacity. If the cost of capital for an all-equity project is 15 percent, what is the adjusted cost of capital? Assume MM's Proposition I corrected for taxes holds, and that the corporate tax rate is 35 percent.
   a. 12.0 percent.
* b. 13.4 percent.
   c. 14.8 percent.
   d. 15.0 percent.
   e. None of the above.

14. A project costs $200 million, offers a perpetual cash flow stream, and adds $50 million to the firm's debt capacity. If the cost of capital for an all-equity project is 17 percent, what is the adjusted cost of capital? Assume MM's Proposition I corrected for taxes holds, and that the corporate tax rate is 35 percent.
   a. 17.0 percent.
   b. 12.5 percent.
* c. 15.5 percent.
   d. 16.1 percent.
   e. None of the above.

15. A project costs $10 million and is expected to produce net cash flows of $1 million a year in perpetuity. The opportunity cost of capital is 12 percent. If the project adds $5 million to debt capacity and MM's Proposition I corrected for taxes holds, what is the project's APV? The corporate tax rate is 35 percent.
   a. -$1,667,000
   b. $5,000,000
   c. $1,800,000
* d. $ 101,000
   e. None of the above.

16. A project costs $80 million and is expected to produce an annual pretax cash flow of $9.09 million in perpetuity. The corporate tax rate is 35 percent. The cost of capital for an all-equity-financed project is 10 percent, but the project adds $20 million to the firm's debt capacity. What is the project's NPV using the MM adjusted cost of capital formula?
* a. -$15.25 million
   b. $19.62 million
   c. -$45.13 million
   d. $88.81 million
   e. None of the above.

17. A firm is proposing to undertake a scale expansion. It would cost $40 million and produce an expected cash flow of $8 million a year in perpetuity before tax at 35 percent. The firm is financed 40 percent by debt. The expected return on the firm's equity is 20 percent, and the interest rate on its debt is 12 percent. What is the NPV of the project using the weighted average cost of capital?
    a. -$21.48 million.
    b. $12.91 million.
    c. -$ 9.05 million.
*   d. -$ 5.61 million.
    e. None of the above.

18. Look back at question 17. If you assume the MM adjusted cost of capital formula is correct, what is the required rate of return if the project is all-equity financed?
    a. 13.11 percent.
*   b. 17.58 percent.
    c. 15.87 percent.
    d. 20.00 percent.
    e. None of the above.

19. When a project is not a perpetuity, what bias (if any) results from using the MM formula?
*   a. The MM formula overestimates NPV.
    b. The MM formula underestimates NPV.
    c. Can't say.

20. Risk-free cash flows should be discounted at the after-tax interest rate:
    a. Only if Miller's theory of debt and taxes holds.
    b. Only if MM's Proposition I corrected for taxes holds.
*   c. Regardless of whether the Miller or MM theorems are correct.
    d. Never.

Chapter 19 - True-False Questions

T   1.   If a project offers an internal rate of return of 9 percent and the adjusted cost of capital is 8.5 percent, the adjusted present value is positive.

F   2.   The adjusted cost of capital reflects only the firm's business risk.

T   3.   The MM formula for the adjusted cost of capital assumes that the only side effect is the interest tax shield on debt.

F   4.   The MM formula for the adjusted cost of capital is strictly correct only for one-year projects.

T   5.   The weighted average cost of capital formula states that the adjusted cost of capital is a weighted average of the expected return on the firm's equity and the after-tax return on its debt.

F   6.   The MM formula expresses the adjusted cost of capital as a function of the expected return on levered equity, the corporate tax rate, and the project's contribution to debt capacity.

T   7.   The Miles-Ezzell adjusted cost of capital formula assumes the firm adjusts its borrowing to maintain a constant debt-to-value ratio.

F   8.   When calculating the weighted average cost of capital, one should use the book values of debt and equity.

T   9.   The "textbook" weighted average cost of capital can be used to discount project cash flows if the project has the same business risk as the firm as a whole.

F   10.   The weighted average cost of capital depends on the immediate source of funds for the project.

T   11.   When using the adjusted present value rule, base-case NPV is calculated by discounting project cash flows at a rate that reflects the project's business risk.

F   12.   Issue costs do not affect adjusted present values.

T   13.   Generally speaking, tangible assets whose value is relatively independent of the firm's fortunes make an above-average addition to the firm's debt capacity.

F   14.   All projects make the same contribution to debt capacity.

T   15. Adjusted present value equals base-case NPV plus the sum of the present values of any financing side effects.

F   16. The adjusted present value rule states that the firm should accept a project if the adjusted present value is at least as great as base-case NPV.

T   17. Discounting at the weighted average cost of capital assumes that debt is rebalanced every period to maintain a constant ratio of debt to the market value of the firm.

F   18. For any particular project, the "opportunity cost of capital" and the "adjusted cost of capital" are the same.

T   19. Safe, nominal cash flows are valued by discounting at the after-tax borrowing rate.

F   20. Of all the cost of capital formulas, the one used the most is that of Miles and Ezzell.

T   21. It does not matter whether you calculate a project's APV or calculate its NPV using the adjusted cost of capital; the answers will be the same.

F   22. Safe, nominal cash flows are valued by discounting at the firm's pre-tax borrowing rate.

T   23. If Miller's "Debt and Taxes" is correct, the required return on risk-free equity is the net-of-tax interest rate. If MM are correct, the adjusted cost of capital for a risk-free project is also the net-of-tax interest rate. In either case, risk-free cash flows should be discounted at the net-of-tax interest rate.

Chapter 19 - Essay Questions

1. Discuss the advantages and limitations of using the weighted average cost of capital as a discount rate to evaluate capital budgeting projects.

Answer

The weighted average cost of capital has the advantages of being relatively simple to calculate, use, and explain to those not well-versed in finance. It has the disadvantage that it applies only to those projects that have a business risk the same as the firm's and so is invalid for projects whose business risk differs substantially from that of the firm as a whole.

2. Under what circumstances would it be better to use the Adjusted Present Value (APV) approach instead of the weighted average cost of capital (WACC) approach to valuing a project?

Answer

The WACC approach takes into account the tax effects on interest payments but does not incorporate any other financing side effects. Thus, if these side effects are important - substantial issue costs for equity, or perhaps a below-market-rate financing rate offered by some government agency - then the APV approach should be used.

Chapter 20 - Multiple Choice Questions

1. Which of the following is/are call options?
   a. The abandonment option on an investment project.
   b. Stand-by underwriting.
   c. a and b.
   * d. The company's option to redeem its bonds at a premium before maturity.
   e. None of the above.

2. Suppose an investor sells a put option. What will happen if the stock price on the exercise date exceeds the exercise price?
   a. The seller will need to deliver stock to the owner of the option.
   b. The seller will be obliged to buy stock from the owner of the option.
   * c. The owner will not exercise his option.
   d. None of the above.

3. Which of the following investors would be happy to see the stock price rise sharply?
   a. Investor who owns the stock and a put option.
   b. Investor who has sold a put option.
   c. Investor who owns the stock and has sold a call option.
   d. Investor who has sold a call option.
   * e. a and b.

4. Which of the following investors would be happy to see the stock price rise sharply?
   * a. Investor who owns a call option.
   b. Investor who owns a put option.
   c. Investor who owns the stock and has sold a call option.
   d. Investor who has sold a call option.
   e. None of the above.

5. Suppose an investor buys one share of stock and a put option on the stock. What will be the value of her investment on the final exercise date if the stock price is below the exercise price?
   a. The value of two shares of stock.
   b. The value of one share of stock plus the exercise price.
   * c. The exercise price.
   d. The value of one share of stock minus the exercise price.

6. For European options, the value of a call plus the present value of the exercise price is equal to:
   a. The value of a put minus the value of a share.
 * b. The value of a put plus the value of a share.
   c. The value of a share minus the value of a call.
   d. The value of a share minus the value of a put.

7. For European options, the value of a call minus the value of a put is equal to:
   a. The present value of the exercise price minus the value of a share.
   b. The present value of the exercise price plus the value of a share.
   c. The value of a share plus the present value of the exercise price.
 * d. The value of a share minus the present value of the exercise price.

8. For European options, the value of a put is equal to:
 * a. The value of a call minus the value of a share plus the present value of the exercise price.
   b. The value of a call plus the value of a share plus the present value of the exercise price.
   c. The value of the share minus the value of a call plus the present value of the exercise price.
   d. The value of the share minus the present value of the exercise price plus the value of a call.

9. Suppose an investor buys one share of stock and a put option on the stock and simultaneously sells a call option on the stock with the same exercise price. What will be the value of his investment on the final exercise date?
   a. Above the exercise price if the stock price rises and below the exercise price if it falls.
 * b. Equal to the exercise price regardless of the stock price.
   c. Equal to zero regardless of the stock price.
   d. Below the exercise price if the stock price rises and above if it falls.

10. Suppose you buy a call and lend the present value of its exercise price. You could match the payoffs of this strategy by:
   a. Buying stock and selling a call.
   b. Selling a put and lending the present value of the exercise price.
   c. Buying stock and selling a put.
 * d. Buying stock and buying a put.

11. Which of the following describes the difference between the value of a U.S. Treasury bond and a risky corporate bond?
    a. The value of a call option on the firm's assets with an exercise price equal to the face value of the bonds.
    * b. The value of a put option on the firm's assets with an exercise price equal to the face value of the bonds.
    c. The value of the firm's assets minus the value of a put option on the assets with an exercise price equal to the face value of the bonds.
    d. The value of the firm's assets minus the value of a call option on the assets with an exercise price equal to the face value of the bonds.

12. Which of the following features increase(s) the value of a call option?
    a. A high interest rate.
    b. A long time to maturity.
    c. A highly variable stock price.
    * d. All of the above.

13. Relative to the underlying stock, a call option always has:
    * a. A higher beta and a higher standard deviation of return.
    b. A lower beta and a higher standard deviation of return.
    c. A higher beta and a lower standard deviation of return.
    d. A lower beta and a lower standard deviation of return.

14. The option delta is calculated as the ratio of:
    a. The spread of possible share prices to the spread of possible option prices.
    b. The share price to the option price.
    * c. The spread of possible option prices to the spread of possible share prices.
    d. The option price to the share price.
    e. None of the above.

15. A call option has an exercise price of $150. At the final exercise date, the stock price could be either $100 or $200. Which investment would combine to give the same payoff as the stock?
    * a. Lend PV of $100 and buy two calls.
    b. Lend PV of $100 and sell two calls.
    c. Borrow $100 and buy two calls.
    d. Borrow $100 and sell two calls.
    e. None of the above.

16. Suppose Ralph's stock price is currently $50. In the next six months it will either fall to $40 or rise to $80. What is the option delta of a call option with an exercise price of $50?
    a. 0
    b. .375
    c. .500
    d. .625
*   e. .75

17. Suppose Fred's stock price is currently $70. In the next six months it will either fall to $60 or rise to $90. What is the option delta of a call option with an exercise price of $65?
    a. .278
    b. .417
*   c. .833
    d. .925
    e. 1.00

18. Suppose Waldo's stock price is currently $50. In the next six months it will either fall to $40 or rise to $80. What is the current value of a six-month call option with an exercise price of $50? The six-month risk-free interest rate is 2%.
    a. $30.00
    b. $ 2.40
    c. $15.00
    d. $ 8.25
*   e. $ 8.09

19. Suppose Ann's stock price is currently $25. In the next six months it will either fall to $15 or rise to $40. What is the current value of a six-month call option with an exercise price of $20? The six-month risk-free interest rate is 5%.
    a. $20.00
*   b. $ 8.57
    c. $ 9.52
    d. $13.10
    e. $ 9.00

20. Suppose Carol's stock price is currently $20. In the next six months it will either fall to $10 or rise to $40. What is the current value of a six-month call option with an exercise price of $12? The six-month risk-free interest rate is 5%.
* a. $ 9.79
  b. $10.28
  c. $16.88
  d. $13.33
  e. $20.00

21. Which of the following inputs is not needed to use the Black-Scholes formula?
  a. Risk-free interest rate.
  b. Exercise price.
  c. Time to maturity.
* d. Beta of the stock.
  e. Standard deviation of the stock.

Chapter 20 - True-False Questions

T   1.   A call option gives its owner the right to buy stock at a fixed exercise price.

F   2.   If you write a put option, you acquire the right to sell stock at a fixed exercise price.

T   3.   When a firm borrows, lenders in effect acquire the company, and the shareholders receive an option to buy it back for the face value of the debt.

F   4.   A European option gives its owner the right to exercise the option at any time before the final exercise date.

T   5.   The writer of a put option loses if the stock price declines.

F   6.   In the case of an American option the writer decides if and when to exercise.

T   7.   An investor who has an option to buy stock and enough money in the bank to exercise the option is in the same position as an investor who owns the stock plus an option to sell it.

F   8.   If, the day a call option expires, the stock price is above the exercise price, the option is worth the stock price plus the exercise price.

T   9.   A call option provides the investor with leverage - the investor has to pay the call's purchase price today but does not need to pay the exercise price until later.

F   10.   An option buyer can turn himself into an option writer by appropriately buying or selling stock and borrowing or lending money.

T   11.   For European options,
Value of call = share price + value of put − PV(exercise price)

F   12.   For European options,
Value of call = share price − value of put + PV(exercise price)

T   13.   The value of limited liability is the value of a put on the firm's assets with an exercise price equal to the promised payment to bondholders.

F   14. Bond value = PV(promised payment to bondholders)
                      + value of put

T   15. Any set of contingent payoffs - that is, payoffs which depend on the value of some other asset - can be valued as a mixture of simple options on that asset.

F   16. The value of a call option decreases as the rate of interest and time to maturity increase.

T   17. The value of an option increases with the variability of the stock price.

F   18. The key parameter in valuing a call option is the expected rate of return on the underlying common stock.

T   19. A call option is always riskier than the underlying stock.

F   20. If investors expect a high return from the stock, the value of the call option will be high, relative to the stock price, and the value of the put will be low.

T   21. The risk of a call option changes every time the price of the underlying stock changes.

F   22. The risk-neutral method of option valuation works because investors can hold a diversified portfolio of options and thereby eliminate virtually all non-market risk.

T   23. It is possible to replicate an investment in a call option by a levered investment in the underlying asset.

F   24. One key variable in the Black-Scholes formula is the expected return on the underlying stock.

T   25. The risk-neutral method values a call as if the expected rate of return on the underlying share were the risk-free interest rate.

Chapter 20 - Essay Questions

1. Discuss how options may be used to better understand the relationship between the value of a firm's debt and the value of its equity.

Answer

With limited liability, a firm's stockholders have the option to default; that is, they have the option not to make a bond payment. In other words, we may think of the stockholders as having a call option on the firm's assets - if they exercise this option (i.e., make the bond payment), they own the firm's assets; if they fail to exercise this option, the firm belongs to the bondholders. It follows that the bonds are worth the asset value of the firm less the value of the stockholders' option to default.

2. Discuss those factors which determine the value of a call option.

Answer

The value of a call option is determined by five factors; we will discuss the effect of each, assuming the others are held constant.
First, the stock price. The higher the stock price, the more valuable the option. Second, the higher the exercise price, the lower the value of the option. This is because the exercise price is what must be paid to acquire the stock. Third, the interest rate. This is because, when the stock price is high compared to the exercise price, buying a call is like purchasing a stock but financing part of the purchase price. So, the higher the interest rate, the more valuable the option. Fourth, time to maturity. The longer the time until the option matures, the greater the possibility that the stock price will exceed the exercise price and the more valuable the option. Fifth, the variability of the stock price. This is because the greater the variability, the greater the potential payoff from the option, hence the more valuable the option.

Chapter 21 - Multiple Choice Questions

1. It is not possible to use standard discounted cash flow analysis to value options because:
    a. This is wrong; discounted cash flow analysis may be used to correctly value options.
    * b. The discount rate changes as the value of the underlying asset changes.
    c. The time horizon for options is variable.
    d. The risk-free rate is not always applicable.
    e. None of the above.

2. The value of a business that might suffer from declining profitability is equal to:
    a. The value of the abandonment call option.
    b. The value of the business without the abandonment option.
    c. The value of the abandonment put option.
    d. A and B.
    * e. B and C.

3. If e is base of natural logarithms, σ the standard deviation of continuously compounded annual returns on the asset, and h the interval as a fraction of a year, then the quantity {1 + upside change} is equal to:
    * a. $e^{\sigma\sqrt{h}}$
    b. $e^{h\sqrt{\sigma}}$
    c. $\sigma e^{\sqrt{h}}$
    d. $h e^{\sqrt{\sigma}}$
    e. None of the above.

4. If u equals the quantity {1 + upside change}, then the quantity {1 + downside change} is equal to:
    a. $-u$
    b. $-1/u$
    * c. $1/u$
    d. $1/(2u)$
    e. None of the above.

5. If the standard deviation of continuously compounded annual returns on the asset is 40% and the interval is a year, then the upside change is equal to:
    a. 88.2%
    b. 8.7%
    c. 63.2%
    * d. 49.2%
    e. 37.7%

6. If the standard deviation of continuously compounded annual returns on the asset is 40% and the interval is a year, then the downside change is equal to:
    a. 27.4%
    b. 53.6%
*   c. 33.0%
    d. 38.7%
    e. 46.9%

7. If the standard deviation of continuously compounded annual returns on the asset is 20% and the interval is half a year, then the upside change is equal to:
*   a. 15.2%
    b. 40.6%
    c. 25.1%
    d. 37.9%
    e. 61.1%

8. If the standard deviation of continuously compounded annual returns on the asset is 20% and the interval is half a year, then the downside change is equal to:
    a. 27.5%
    b. 37.9%
    c. 19.3%
    d. 20.1%
*   e. 13.2%

9. Which of the following conditions might lead a financial manager to delay a positive-NPV investment project? Assume project NPV if undertaken immediately is held constant.
    a. The risk-free interest rate falls.
*   b. Uncertainty about future project value increases.
    c. The first cash inflow generated by the project is lower than previously thought.
    d. Investment required for the project increases.
    e. There is never any reason to delay a positive-NPV project.

10. Which of the following conditions might lead a financial manager to decide to expedite a positive Net Present Value investment project that previously she had decided to delay?
    a. The risk-free interest rate falls.
    b. Uncertainty about future project value increases.
    c. The first cash inflow generated by the project is lower than previously thought.
*   d. Uncertainty about future project value decreases.
    e. Investment required for the project increases.

11. Here is an unusual option. Suppose you have a plot of vacant land which could be used for the construction of a supermarket or a massage parlor. Is this:
    a. Equal to a call option on each of the two assets?
    b. More valuable than an option to buy each of the two assets?
    c. Equal to an option to buy the more variable asset?
*   d. None of the above.

12. Consider the following situation:
    A business produces net cash flows of \$400,000 per year. There is no upward or downward trend in the cash flows, but there is some year-to-year variation, with an annual standard deviation of 20 percent. The real estate occupied by the business is owned and could be sold for \$1,000,000. Ignore taxes.

In the language of options, this situation is equivalent to:
*   a. An American put option to abandon the restaurant at an exercise price of \$1 million. The restaurant's current value is \$400,000/r. The annual standard deviation of the changes in the value of the restaurant as a going concern is 20 percent.
    b. A European put option to abandon the restaurant at an exercise price of \$1 million. The restaurant's current value is \$400,000/r. The annual standard deviation of the changes in the value of the restaurant as a going concern is 20 percent.
    c. An American call option to abandon the restaurant at an exercise price of \$1 million. The restaurant's current value is \$400,000/r. The annual standard deviation of the changes in the value of the restaurant as a going concern is 20 percent.
    d. A European call option to abandon the restaurant at an exercise price of \$1 million. The restaurant's current value is \$400,000/r. The annual standard deviation of the changes in the value of the restaurant as a going concern is 20 percent.

13. You can use options to replicate a short position in the asset by:
    a. Selling a put, buying a call, and lending the balance.
    b. Buying a put, selling a call, and borrowing the balance.
    c. Selling a put, selling a call, and lending the balance.
*   d. Buying a put, selling a call, and lending the balance.
    e. None of the above.

14. You can ensure against a fall in the value of an asset by:
    a. Buying the asset and selling a put.
*   b. Buying the asset and buying a put.
    c. Selling the asset and buying a put.
    d. Buying the asset and buying a call.
    e. None of the above.

15. An example of a real option is:
    a. The option to make follow-on investments.
    b. The option to abandon a project.
    c. The option to wait before investing.
    d. A and C.
  * e. A, B, and C.

16. In terms of a real option, the cash flows from the project play the same role as:
    a. The stock price.
    b. The exercise price.
  * c. The dividends.
    d. The variance.
    e. None of the above.

17. A rational manager may be reluctant to commit to a positive Net Present Value project when:
    a. This is wrong: A rational manager is always willing to commit to a positive Net Present Value project.
    b. The value of the option to abandon is high.
    c. The exercise price is high.
    d. The opportunity cost of capital is high.
  * e. The value of the option to wait is high.

18. Production facilities that are flexible in terms of possible raw materials used are most valuable when:
    a. Product demand is highly volatile.
    b. Product price is highly volatile.
  * c. Raw material prices are highly volatile.
    d. Labor costs are highly volatile.
    e. All of the above.

19. Consider an electric utility that may use either coal or natural gas to generate electricity. Under which of the following conditions would it be most valuable to have cofiring equipment? Let σ_C be the annual standard deviation of coal prices, σ_N be the annual standard deviation of natural gas prices, and ρ the correlation between coal prices and natural gas prices.
  * a. σ_C high, σ_N high, ρ low.
    b. σ_C high, σ_N low, ρ low.
    c. σ_C low, σ_N high, ρ low.
    d. σ_C low, σ_N low, ρ high.
    e. All of the above: cofiring equipment is always valuable.

20. Consider an electric utility that may use either coal or natural gas to generate electricity. Under which of the following conditions would it be least valuable to have cofiring equipment? Let σ_C be the annual standard deviation of coal prices, σ_N be the annual standard deviation of natural gas prices, and ρ the correlation between coal prices and natural gas prices.
    a. σ_C high, σ_N high, ρ low.
    b. σ_C high, σ_N low, ρ low.
    c. σ_C low, σ_N high, ρ low.
*   d. σ_C low, σ_N low, ρ high.
    e. None of the above: Cofiring equipment is always valuable.

Chapter 21 - True-False Questions

T   1.   The opportunity to undertake a positive-NPV capital investment is like owning an in-the-money call option.

F   2.   The option to abandon a project can be valued as a call option.

T   3.   Discounted cash flow (DCF) analysis implicitly assumes that real assets are held passively. As a consequence, DCF analysis ignores the value of real options.

F   4.   It is possible to use standard discounted cash flow analysis to value an option.

T   5.   As the number of intervals is increased, the values obtained from the binomial method will converge to the Black-Scholes equation value.

F   6.   Any project with a negative Net Present Value, calculated from the anticipated cash flows, should never be considered by a company.

T   7.   It is sometimes rational to consider waiting to make a decision about investing in a project whose Net Present Value is currently negative.

F   8.   Because call options are "worth more alive than dead" and because the opportunity to invest in a project may be considered to be a call option, companies should never invest in a project unless they face an "invest now or never" situation.

T   9.   The positive cash flows from an investment play the same role as dividend payments on common stock.

F   10.   The binomial method of option valuation may be thought of as an application of decision trees.

T   11.   When an asset does not pay dividends, an American call option is always worth more alive than dead.

F   12.   A European put is worth more than an American put.

T   13.   It is better to exercise a call option on the with-dividend date instead of the ex-dividend date.

F   14.   It is better to exercise a put option on the with-dividend date instead of the ex-dividend date.

T   15.   The option to wait before investing in a project is an example of a real option.

F   16.   The option to invest in the common stock of a steel-producing company is an example of a real option.

T   17.   Because the Black-Scholes formula does not allow for early exercise, it cannot be used to value an American put exactly.

F   18.   The Black-Scholes option pricing formula may be derived from the Capital Asset Pricing Model.

T   19.   When using the Black-Scholes formula to value a European call on a dividend-paying stock, you should reduce the price of the stock by the present value of dividends paid before the option's maturity. For real options, the procedure is the same, except that for real options the "dividends" are the cash flows generated by the asset.

F   20.   Valuing a real option by the risk-neutral method is not the same as valuing the option as if it were traded.

Chapter 21 - Essay Questions

1. Discuss the usefulness of considering the options inherent in any capital budgeting project.

<u>Answer</u>

Traditional Net Present Value, or Discounted Cash Flow, analysis is incomplete in most capital budgeting situations because it implicitly assumes that the firm is passive, i.e., that once the investment decision is made the firm can do nothing. This ignores, for example, the possibility of follow-on investments as well as the possibility of abandoning the project. These real options are important and have value, and thus should be taken into account when the project is initially analyzed.

2. When should a rational manager consider postponing investment in a project with a positive Net Present Value?

<u>Answer</u>

One of the interesting things that comes out of applying option pricing theory to capital budgeting decisions is that under certain conditions the option to wait may be very valuable. If the project in question currently has a positive Net Present Value but also has a high volatility, the project may be worth significantly more or significantly less in the future. The value of waiting for the uncertainty to be resolved may outweigh the value of undertaking the project immediately.

Chapter 22 - Multiple Choice Questions

1. Warrants are sometimes issued:
   a. With private placement bonds.
   b. To investment bankers as compensation.
   c. To creditors in the event of bankruptcy.
   d. To common stock holders.
* e. All of the above.

2. The "theoretical value" of a warrant means:
   a. Zero.
   b. The stock price.
* c. The lower limit of the warrant's value.
   d. The current price of the warrant.
   e. None of the above.

3. Every time a dividend is paid on the common stock, the warrant holder:
   a. Gains value.
* b. Loses value.
   c. Is unaffected.
   d. May either gain or lose, depending on other factors, such as stock price volatility.

4. A Standard Oil Company of Virginia warrant gives its owner the right to buy one share of common stock anytime in the next three years at a price of $35. The common stock price is currently $38 and the warrant price is $9. What is the theoretical value (i.e., lower limit) of the warrant?
   a. $0
* b. $3
   c. $6
   d. $9
   e. None of the above.

5. Standard Oil Company of Florida has 200,000 shares outstanding and 50,000 warrants. Each warrant entitles its owner to buy one share anytime in the next two years at a price of $20. Undiluted earnings per share are $2.40. What are diluted earnings per share?
* a. $1.92
   b. $1.80
   c. $1.20
   d. $2.40
   e. None of the above.

6. A Standard Oil Company of Nebraska warrant gives its owner the right to buy one share of common stock anytime in the next three years at a price of $74. The common stock price is currently $80 and the warrant price is $14. What is the theoretical value (i.e., lower limit) of the warrant?
   a. $0
   b. $10
* c. $6
   d. $14
   e. None of the above.

7. Standard Oil Company of Maine has 400,000 shares outstanding and 80,000 warrants. Each warrant entitles its owner to buy one share anytime in the next two years at a price of $10. Undiluted earnings per share are $6.73. What are diluted earnings per share?
   a. $6.73
   b. $3.37
   c. $2.38
* d. $5.61
   e. None of the above.

8. Standard Oil Company of Georgia has 300,000 shares outstanding and has just issued 320,000 warrants. Each warrant entitles its owner to buy one share anytime in the next year at a price of $20. The common stock price is currently $25; the warrant sale price was $10. The value of each warrant is equal to $1/(1 + q)$ = .484 call options on an alternative firm. What would the share price of that alternative firm be?
   a. $17.26
   b. $25.00
* c. $35.67
   d. $38.00
   e. $40.00

9. Standard Oil Company of Oregon has 500,000 shares outstanding and has just issued 200,000 warrants. Each warrant entitles its owner to buy one share anytime in the next year at a price of $30. The common stock price is currently $40; the warrant sale price was $15. The value of each warrant is equal to $1/(1 + q)$ = .714 call options on an alternative firm. What would the share price of that alternative firm be?
   a. $15.00
   b. $25.00
   c. $28.56
   d. $32.86
* e. $46.00

10. Eastinghouse common stock is currently priced at $30, and its 8 percent Convertible Debenture is priced at 85 percent. Each debenture can be converted into 25 shares of common stock before 1994. What is the conversion price?
    a. $30.00
    b. $34.00
*   c. $40.00
    d. $43.40
    e. None of the above.

11. Consolidated Cake's common stock is currently priced at $15, and its 10 percent Convertible Debenture is priced at 90 percent. The conversion price is $20. What is the conversion ratio?
    a. .9
    b. 2
    c. 5
    d. 45
*   e. None of the above.

12. Look again at question 5. Suppose that the company can call the bond at 105. If the company and bondholders act rationally, what will be the stock price at which investors will convert?
    a. $20
*   b. $21
    c. $25
    d. $19
    e. $15

13. Consolidated Fruit's common stock is currently priced at $25, and its 15 percent Convertible Debenture is priced at 85 percent. The conversion price is $40. What is the conversion ratio?
*   a. 25
    b. 20
    c. 50
    d. 45
    e. None of the above.

14. Look again at question 13. Suppose that the company can call the bond at 110. If the company and bondholders act rationally, what will be the stock price at which investors will convert?
    a. $50
    b. $41
    c. $40
*   d. $44
    e. $50

15. A LYON is a bond which:
    a. Is callable.
    b. Is putable.
    c. Is convertible.
    d. Has a zero coupon.
*   e. All of the above.

16. A warrant with a $5 exercise price is issued when the stock price is $3.50. Two years later, the warrant is exercised after the stock price has increased to $8.
    a. The company has won. It ended up issuing stock at $5 (the exercise price), rather than at the $3.50 stock price prevailing when the warrants were issued.
*   b. The company has lost. It ended up issuing shares at $5 when it could have issued them at $8.

17. Which of the following could be a sensible reason for issuing convertibles?
*   a. Convertibles are convenient and flexible - they're usually unsecured and subordinated, and cash requirements for debt service are relatively low.
    b. Interest rates on convertible issues are significantly less than on straight debt.
    c. Firms that need equity capital use convertibles as a roundabout way of issuing stock.
    d. Firms prefer to issue convertibles when their shares are under-valued.
    e. None of the above - there are no sensible reasons for issuing convertibles.

18. Compared to convertibles, warrants are typically:
    a. Issued privately.
    b. Exercised for cash.
    c. Detachable from the associated financial instrument.
*   d. All of the above.
    e. None of the above.

19. Reasons why companies might reasonably issue convertible debt include:
*   a. The company is growing rapidly and needs a temporary source of cheap financing.
    b. It represents cheap debt.
    c. It is a good way to defer the issuance of equity.
    d. All of the above.
    e. None of the above.

20. Fred's Super Stores has issued $10 million of a 10 percent subordinated debenture; this represents 10,000 bonds, each with a face value of $1,000. Fred's net income is $30 million, the current number of shares outstanding is 3 million, the bond's conversion ratio is 40, and the firm's tax rate is 35%. On a fully diluted basis, earnings per share is:
    a. $10.00
    b. $9.23
* c. $9.01
    d. $8.93
    e. $8.82

Chapter 22 - True-False Questions

F   1.   A warrant holder is not entitled to vote but does receive any cash dividends.

T   2.   If there is a stock split, an adjustment is made both to the number of shares to which the warrant holder is entitled and to the exercise price of the warrants.

F   3.   The difference between the stock price and the warrant price is often termed the "theoretical value" of the warrant.

T   4.   The owner of a warrant loses every time a dividend is paid on the underlying common stock.

F   5.   Because a warrant is like a call option, it never pays to exercise a warrant before maturity.

T   6.   The problem of dilution never arises with call options but does arise with warrants.

F   7.   If a debenture is convertible into 25 shares of common stock, the conversion ratio is 1000/25 = 40.

T   8.   If a debenture is convertible into 25 shares of common stock, the conversion value is 1000/25 = $40.

F   9.   Warrant holders are usually protected against stock splits and stock dividends but convertible holders are not.

T   10. The owner of a convertible bond owns both a bond and a call option.

F   11. A convertible debenture cannot be worth more than its conversion value or less than its bond value.

T   12. Owners of convertible bonds miss out on dividends paid to common stock.

F   13. LYONs are found only in the zoo.

T   14. Firms often do not call their convertibles until they are worth much (say, about 20%) more than their call price.

F   15. Both warrants and convertible bonds are exercised for cash.

T   16. Warrants are not usually callable, though the company may tempt warrant holders to exercise by offering a temporary reduction in the exercise price.

F   17. Warrants are rarely issued as part of a private placement.

T   18. Warrants may be issued on their own, that is, as a separate security in their own right.

F   19. Convertible debt represents a way for a company to issue cheap (to the company) debt.

T   20. Issuing convertible debt makes sense whenever investors would have difficulty estimating the risk of the company's bonds.

Chapter 22 - Essay Questions

1. Discuss the valuation of a convertible bond.

Answer
A convertible bond may be thought of as having two components, a bond value and a conversion value. At maturity, the value of the bond will be the greater of the bond value or the conversion value. That is, if it is the best interests of the bondholders to convert, they will do so; if the bondholders are better off retaining the bond, they will do that. Before maturity, the conversion value will be generally positive, and so the convertible will always be worth more than the bond value.

2. Discuss the differences between warrants and convertibles.

Answer
The main differences are that: (1) warrants are usually issued as part of a private placement; (2) warrants can be detached, or separated, from the accompanying financial instrument and sold separately; (3) warrants may be issued by themselves; (4) warrants are exercised for cash and thus have different effects on the company's cash flow and capital structure; and (5) warrants and convertibles are subject to different tax rules.

3. Discuss why managers issue convertible debt.

Answer
One invalid reason for issuing convertible debt is that it represents cheap debt: Such reasoning ignores the value of the option included with the bond. Another invalid reason is to defer the issue of equity: The bonds may never be converted, and so this is an unreliable way to issue equity.
Issuing convertible debt does make sense in situations where it is difficult for investors to correctly assess the risk of a company's debt, where investors are worried that management may not act in the best interests of the bondholders, or when companies need cheap immediate financing and are willing to trade this for equity issued at a later date.

Chapter 23 - Multiple Choice Questions

1. Suppose that the expected inflation rate is 5 percent and the nominal interest rate is 10 percent. According to Fisher's theory, what would be the consequence of a rise in the expected inflation rate to 15 percent?
    a. Increase the real rate to approximately 15 percent.
*   b. Increase the nominal rate to approximately 20 percent.
    c. Leave the nominal interest rate unchanged.
    d. Reduce the real rate to negative 5 percent.

2. Suppose that the expected inflation rate is 50 percent and the nominal interest rate is 60 percent. According to Fisher's theory, what would be the consequence of a rise in the expected inflation rate to 75 percent?
*   a. Increase the nominal rate to approximately 87 percent.
    b. Increase the real rate to approximately 25 percent.
    c. Reduce the real rate to negative 15 percent.
    d. Leave the nominal interest rate unchanged.

3. An example of a stripped bond is a:
    a. Treasury Investment Growth Receipts.
    b. Certificate of Accrual on Treasury Securities.
*   c. Both of the above.
    d. None of the above.

4. Consider a bond with a face value of $1,000, a coupon rate of 6 percent, a yield to maturity of 8 percent, and ten years to maturity. This bond's duration is:
    a. 8.7 years.
    b. 6.5 years.
    c. 0.1 years.
*   d. 7.6 years.
    e. 10.0 years.

5. Consider a bond with a face value of $1,000, a coupon rate of 7 percent, a yield to maturity of 10 percent, and twenty years to maturity. This bond's duration is:
*   a. 10.0 years.
    b. 7.4 years.
    c. 0.1 years.
    d. 12.6 years.
    e. 20.0 years.

6. Consider a bond with a face value of $1,000, a coupon rate of 0 percent, a yield to maturity of 9 percent, and ten years to maturity. This bond's duration is:
   a. 6.7 years.
   b. 7.5 years.
   c. 0.1 years.
   d. 9.6 years.
 * e. 10.0 years.

7. Consider a bond with a duration of 15.5 years and a yield of 6 percent. This bond's volatility is:
   a. 9.3 percent.
   b. 6.8 percent.
 * c. 14.6 percent.
   d. 6.0 percent.

8. Consider a bond with a duration of 5.7 years and a yield of 9 percent. This bond's volatility is:
   a. 1.9 percent.
 * b. 5.2 percent.
   c. 5.1 percent.
   d. 9.0 percent.

9. If the 3-year spot rate is 12 percent and the 2-year spot rate is 10 percent, what is the forward rate of interest?
   a. 1.8 percent.
   b. 3.7 percent.
 * c. 16.1 percent.
   d. 9.5 percent.
   e. None of the above.

10. If the 5-year spot rate is 10 percent and the 4-year spot rate is 9 percent, what is the forward rate of interest?
 * a. 14.1 percent.
   b. .9 percent.
   c. 1.0 percent.
   d. 11.0 percent.
   e. None of the above.

11. If the 4-year spot rate is 7 percent and the 3-year spot rate is 6 percent, what is the forward rate of interest?
   a. 1.0 percent.
 * b. 10.0 percent.
   c. 8.0 percent.
   d. 9.6 percent.
   e. None of the above.

12. If the 20-year forward rate of interest is the same as the 19-year spot rate, what is the 20-year spot rate?
   a. Smaller than the 19-year spot rate.
   b. Larger than the 19-year spot rate.
   c. Can't say without knowing the 21-year spot rate.
* d. The same as the 20-year forward rate.

13. How can one invest today at the 2-year forward rate of interest?
* a. By buying a 2-year bond and selling a 1-year bond with the same coupon.
   b. By buying a 1-year bond and selling a 2-year bond with the same coupon.
   c. By buying a 1-year bond and then after a year reinvesting in a further 1-year bond.

14. $_0r_2$ is the spot interest rate established today on a two-year bond maturing at year 2; $_1r_2$ is the spot interest rate established at year 1 on a one-year bond maturing at year 2, etc. An investor who wants her money back in one year can either buy a one-year bond or buy a two-year bond and sell it after a year. What are the payoffs from a dollar invested in each of these two strategies?

   a. $1 + {_0r_2}$ and $\dfrac{(1 + {_0r_1})(1 + {_0r_2})}{1 + {_1r_2}}$

* b. $1 + {_0r_1}$ and $\dfrac{(1 + {_0r_2})^2}{1 + {_1r_2}}$

   c. $1 + {_0r_1}$ and $\dfrac{(1 + {_0r_1})(1 + {_1r_2})}{1 + {_0r_2}}$

   d. None of the above.

15. See question 14. What does the expectations theory of the term structure imply?
   a. That the expected payoff from investing in the two-year bond for one year must be higher than the expected payoff from the one-year bond to compensate for risk.
   b. That the expected payoff from investing from year 0 to year 1 must be the same as the expected payoff from investing from year 1 to year 2.
* c. That the expected payoff from investing in the two-year bond for one year must be the same as the expected payoff from the one-year bond.
   d. None of the above.

16. If the term structure is downward-sloping, what is the yield to maturity on a 10-year coupon bond?
   a. Lower than the 10-year spot interest rate.
 * b. Greater than the 10-year spot interest rate.
   c. Equal to the 10-year spot rate.
   d. May be above or below the 10-year spot rate.

17. The yield to maturity:
   a. Is the present value of future coupons divided by the present value of the final principal payment.
   b. Is the discount rate at which the present value of promised interest and principal payments equals face value.
   c. Is the discount rate at which the present value of expected interest and principal payments equals market price.
 * d. Is calculated by the same formula as the internal rate of return (IRR).

18. Two bonds mature in 2001, but bond A offers a 10.5 percent yield to maturity, vs. 10.1 percent for bond B. Which of the following explanations makes sense?
   a. The term structure is upward-sloping, and bond A has a higher coupon than B.
   b. The term structure is flat, and bond A offers a higher liquidity premium than bond B.
   c. Bond B has a higher risk of default.
 * d. The term structure is downward-sloping, and bond B has a lower coupon than A.

19. Commercial banks and some other financial institutions are not permitted to invest in bonds unless they are investment grade. What is the definition of an investment grade bond?
   a. One with a triple-A rating.
 * b. One with a rating of Baa or better.
   c. One with a rating of B or better.
   d. One with a rating of C or better.

20. The U.S. government agrees to guarantee a bond issue planned by Demurrage Associates. The value of this guarantee:
   a. Equals the value of a call option on the firm's assets with an exercise price equal to the value of the assets when the guarantee is granted.
   b. Is a subsidy to equity investors in the firm issuing guaranteed debt.
   c. Is a windfall gain to the buyers of the bonds.
   d. Equals the value of a put option on the firm's assets with an exercise price equal to the bond's face value.
 * e. b and d.

Chapter 23 - True-False Questions

T 1. If there is no inflation, the nominal rate of interest is equal to the real rate.

F 2. The supply of capital depends on the amount that firms are willing to invest.

T 3. If investment prospects improve, the interest rate will rise and the level of new investment will increase.

F 4. According to Fama's study of U.S. Treasury bill data, the nominal interest rate provides a biased forecast of the inflation rate.

T 5. Irving Fisher's theory states that the expected real rate of interest is not changed by the expected inflation rate.

F 6. Two bonds with the same maturity but different coupons will always have the same yield to maturity.

T 7. The yield to maturity on a bond is really its internal rate of return.

F 8. A strip is a bond with a constant coupon payment.

T 9. The two-year spot rate of interest is the rate of discount for a cash flow in year two.

F 10. The duration of a bond is the same as its maturity.

T 11. The duration of a zero coupon bond is the same as its maturity.

F 12. The volatility of a bond is a measure of how the bond's yield changes when the term structure shifts.

T 13. If two bonds have the same yield, the bond with the longer duration will have the larger volatility.

F 14. If the one-year spot rate of interest is 8 percent and the two-year spot rate is 9 percent, the forward rate of interest is approximately 8-1/2 percent.

T 15. The usual pattern for the term structure of interest rates is upward sloping, which implies that long-term spot rates are higher than short-term spot rates.

F 16. To calculate the forward rate of interest, you need to know what is going to happen to spot rates.

T 17. The expectations hypothesis implies that the only reason for a declining term structure is that investors expect spot interest rates to fall.

F 18. The expectations hypothesis says that the two-year spot rate of interest equals the expected one-year spot rate.

T 19. The liquidity preference theory says that the forward rate of interest will generally exceed the expected future spot rate.

F 20. The expectations theory of interest rates incorporates risk into the analysis.

T 21. The difference between the forward rate and the expected future spot rate is called the liquidity premium.

F 22. The liquidity premium can never be less than zero.

T 23. Both the expectations theory and the liquidity preference theory of term structure assume that future inflation rates are known.

F 24. If inflation is uncertain, the forward interest rate must equal the expected future spot rate in order to compensate investors for the inflation risk.

T 25. If inflation is uncertain, short-term bonds are generally safer than long-term ones.

F 26. When the probability of default increases, bond prices go up as well as interest rates.

T 27. Holding a corporate bond is equivalent to lending money with no risk of default but at the same time giving stockholders a put option on the firm's assets.

F 28. Investment grade bonds include all bonds rated B or higher.

T 29. The value of a government guarantee of a bond equals the value of a put on the firm's assets.

Chapter 23 - Essay Questions

1. Discuss the concept of duration.

Answer

Duration is one measure of the length of a bond. The most common way to define "length" of a bond, of course, is by its maturity; thus, we speak of, for example, "a twenty-year bond," and so forth. But this is just the length of time until the last payment: Why is this date any more significant than the dates of the other payments? Duration is a measure of length that takes into account all payments; in fact, it is a weighted average of such payments, where the weights are the relative present values.

Duration is a valuable concept for at least two reasons. First, the volatility of a bond is directly related to its duration. Second, one way to hedge financial risk is through a strategy of duration matching.

2. Discuss the theories that attempt to explain the shape of the yield curve.

Answer

There are several theories that attempt to explain the yield curve:

Expectations Hypothesis. This theory postulates that the current forward rates are the expected values of the corresponding future spot rates.

Liquidity Preference Theory. This theory states that, because of uncertainty, investors prefer to invest short term and that borrowers (i.e., issuers of bonds) must offer a forward rate that is higher than the expected future spot rate to sell their bonds. This increment in return is known as the liquidity premium.

Inflation Premium Theory. This theory postulates that, because of uncertainty in the amount of inflation to be experienced in the future, investors will demand a premium; that is, the forward rate will be higher than the expected future spot rate.

The empirical evidence is mixed, but seems to favor the premium theories; precisely which is favored depends on the time period examined.

Chapter 24 - Multiple Choice Questions

1. A "yankee bond" is a bond:
    a. Sold in the United States.
    * b. Sold in the United States by a company from some other country.
    c. Sold by a company from the United States.
    d. Sold in Europe by a company from the United States.
    e. None of the above.

2. A "samurai bond" is a bond:
    a. Sold by a company from Japan.
    b. Sold in the United States by a company from Japan.
    c. Sold in Japan.
    * d. Sold in Japan by a company from some other country.
    e. None of the above.

3. A "Eurobond" is a bond that is:
    a. Sold in Europe.
    b. Sold by underwriters headquartered in London.
    c. Denominated in any European currency, regardless of where the bond is sold.
    d. Denominated in ECUs.
    * e. Sold in a number of foreign countries simultaneously.

4. The most popular currency for Eurobond issues is the:
    a. British pound.
    b. German deutschemark.
    * c. American dollar.
    d. Japanese yen.
    e. Swiss franc.

5. In general:
    a. Bonds issued in the United States are registered.
    b. Bonds issued in the United States are bearer bonds.
    c. Eurobonds are registered.
    d. Eurobonds are bearer bonds.
    * e. A and D.
    f. B and C.

6. In general:
   * a. Bonds issued in the United States pay interest semi-annually, while Eurobonds pay interest annually.
   b. Bonds issued in the United States and Eurobonds pay interest semiannually.
   c. Bonds issued in the United States and Eurobonds pay interest annually.
   d. Bonds issued in the United States pay interest annually, while Eurobonds pay interest semiannually.
   e. None of the above.

7. Which of the following loans is typically secured?
   a. Sinking fund debenture.
   * b. Mortgage bond.
   c. Floating rate note.
   d. Eurobond.
   e. None of the above.

8. Which of the following loans is typically secured?
   * a. Equipment trust certificate.
   b. Debenture.
   c. Floating rate note.
   d. Sinking fund debenture.
   e. None of the above.

9. Which of the following loans is typically not secured?
   a. Collateral trust bond.
   b. Mortgage bond.
   * c. Floating rate note.
   d. Equipment trust certificate.
   e. None of the above.

10. Which of the following provisions would often be included in the indenture for a first-mortgage bond?
    a. A limit on officer salaries.
    b. A negative pledge clause.
    c. A limit on new issues of subordinated debt.
    * d. A limit on the amount of senior debt that can be issued.
    e. All of the above.

11. Which of the following is <u>not</u> an example of an affirmative covenant?
    a. Requirement to maintain a minimum level of working capital.
    b. Requirement to furnish bondholders with a copy of the firm's annual accounts.
    c. Requirement to maintain a minimum level of net worth.
*   d. Requirement to limit dividends to net income.
    e. None of the above.

12. Which of the following features increases the value of a newly issued corporate bond?
    a. The bond is callable.
    b. The bond has an optional sinking fund.
*   c. The bond has a mandatory sinking fund operating by drawings at par.
    d. The bond is a subordinated debenture.
    e. None of the above.

13. Which of the following characteristics typifies private placement bonds?
    a. Are more likely than public issues to contain nonstandard provisions.
    b. Usually involve a simpler contract.
    c. Usually impose more stringent conditions on the borrower.
    d. A and C.
*   e. A, B and C.

14. Which of the following characteristics typifies private placement bonds?
    a. Are less likely than public issues to contain nonstandard provisions.
*   b. Are more easily renegotiated.
    c. Must be registered with the SEC.
    d. Incorporate a sinking fund which purchases bonds in the market.

15. An 8 percent debenture (face value = $1000) pays interest on June 30 and December 31. It is callable at a price of 108 percent together with accrued interest. Suppose the company decides to call the bonds on August 31. What price must it pay for each bond?
    a. $1067
    b. $1080
*   c. $1093
    d. $1100
    e. $1113

16. A 5 percent debenture (face value = $1000) pays interest on June 30 and December 31. It is callable at a price of 105 percent together with accrued interest. Suppose the company decides to call the bonds on September 30. What price must it pay for each bond?
    a. $1000.00
    b. $1037.50
    c. $1050.00
*   d. $1062.50
    e. $1100.00

17. A 7 percent debenture (face value = $1000) pays interest on June 30 and December 31. It is callable at a price of 110 percent together with accrued interest. Suppose the company decides to call the bonds on November 30. What price must it pay for each bond?
*   a. $1129
    b. $1171
    c. $1070
    d. $1100
    e. $1071

18. An 8 percent debenture has 5 years of call protection and is thereafter callable at 100 percent, except that it is non-refundable below interest cost. Which of the following statements is correct?
*   a. The debenture may not be called during the next 5 years.
    b. The debenture may be called any time during the next 5 years.
    c. The lender has the option to demand early repayment.
    d. The bond should be called when the yield on similar non-callable bonds falls to 8 percent.
    e. None of the above.

19. An 8 percent debenture has 5 years of call protection and is thereafter callable at 100 percent, except that it is non-refundable below interest cost. Which of the following statements is correct?
    a. The call price will be less than 100.
*   b. The bond may not be called if the company intends to replace it with another bond yielding less than 8 percent.
    c. The value of the bond will be greater than that of similar non-callable bonds.
    d. The bond price is more variable than that of similar non-callable bonds.
    e. None of the above.

20. Suppose that a company has issued securities with the following face values (figures in thousands):

Common Stock ($1 par value)	$5000
Preferred Stock ($5 par value)	1000
1st Mortgage Bonds	1500
2nd Mortgage Bonds	800
Debentures	3000
Convertible Subordinated Debentures	100

The company has no other liabilities. Mortgaged assets are valued at $2 million and the remaining assets at $1.1 million. In the event of bankruptcy, how much would the holders of the 2nd Mortgage Bonds and of the Debentures each receive if the courts observed strict priority?
- a. $468,000 and $1,755,000.
- b. $800,000 and $ 800,000.
* c. $600,000 and $1,000,000.
- d. $700,000 and $ 900,000.
- e. None of the above.

Chapter 24 - True-False Questions

F 1. The term "yankee bond" refers to any bond sold in the United States.

T 2. A "samurai bond" is a bond sold in Japan by a company from some other country.

F 3. Eurobonds are usually registered.

T 4. Bonds issued in the United States are usually registered.

F 5. Most Eurobonds pay interest semiannually.

T 6. Bond prices are quoted as a percentage of face value.

F 7. Because bonds can generally only be called at a premium, the call provision increases the value of the bond.

T 8. With a bearer bond, the investor must send in coupons to obtain interest payments.

F 9. "Subordinated bond" is just another term for "unsecured bond."

T 10. Sinking funds reduce the average life of a bond and thereby reduce the risk of default.

F 11. Bond indentures never include dividend restrictions.

T 12. Debentures and notes are generally unsecured.

F 13. Indentures for senior debentures usually place restrictions on the amount of subordinated debt that can be issued.

T 14. Usually mortgage bonds are secured by almost all of the company's property.

F 15. The difference between the price of callable bonds and that of non-callable bonds is greatest when bond prices are low.

T 16. Bonds issued by risky companies generally have larger sinking fund requirements.

F 17. Defeasance of a bond issue benefits both stockholders and bondholders.

T   18. Many bond indentures allow the company to acquire bonds for the sinking fund by purchases in the market or by drawing lots for purchase at face value.

F   19. A negative pledge clause states that the company may grant an exclusive lien or claim on any of its assets.

T   20. A company will maximize shareholder wealth if it calls its bonds as soon as the market price reaches the call price.

F   21. Publicly issued bonds are not as highly standardized as privately placed loans.

T   22. Affirmative covenants impose certain duties on the company, e.g., an obligation to maintain a minimum net worth or working capital.

F   23. Private placements usually impose much less stringent conditions on the borrower and these conditions are more easily re-negotiated.

T   24. Private placements usually have a lower fixed issue cost than public offers of debt.

F   25. In most project financing deals, lenders have no recourse to the equity investor if the project fails.

T   26. Project finance requires a capital investment that can be clearly separated from the parent and which offers tangible security to lenders.

Chapter 24 - Essay Questions

1. Discuss the differences between a bond issued only in the United States and a Eurobond.

Answer
There are two primary differences. First, a bond issued in the United States will generally have a fixed rate of interest, while a Eurobond will usually have a floating rate of interest, typically tied to LIBOR. Second, bonds sold in the United States are almost always registered, which means that the owner's name is recorded by the company's registrar; most Eurobonds are sold in bearer form, which means that the certificate itself is the primary evidence of ownership.

2. Discuss the differences between publicly issued bonds and private placements.

Answer
There are three differences. First, publicly issued bonds must be registered with the Securities and Exchange Commission, while private placements need not. Thus, publicly issued bonds require more elaborate contracts and involve higher issue costs (although the interest rate may well be lower). Second, because publicly issued bonds are meant to be traded, they are highly standardized; private placements are tailor-made for the (very few - two or three) companies involved. Third, the restrictions placed on the issuer are much more stringent with a private placement. This is because, if there is a good reason to relax these restrictions, agreement is easily obtained for the private placement; such agreement is almost impossible to obtain with a publicly traded issue.

Chapter 25 - Multiple Choice Questions

1. In addition to the cost of bearing risk, insurance companies also bear:
   a. Administrative costs.
   b. Moral hazard costs.
   c. Adverse selection costs.
* d. All of the above.
   e. None of the above.

2. Insurance companies have some advantages in bearing risk; these include:
   a. Superior ability to estimate the probability of loss.
   b. Extensive experience and knowledge about how to reduce the risk of a loss.
   c. The ability to pool risks and thereby gain from diversification.
   d. None of the above.
* e. All of the above.

3. An example of a derivative security is:
   a. Forward contract.
   b. Future contract.
   c. Option contract.
   d. Swap contract.
* e. All of the above.

4. On November 13, Al buys a July futures contract on 100 tons of soybean meal at a price of $172.0 a ton. On the same day, Bob sells this futures contract at the same price. On November 14, the July contract is trading at $174.2 a ton. Given that the contract is marked to market, what payments need to be made on the 14th?
   a. Al pays the clearing house $220 and the clearing house pays Bob $220.
* b. Bob pays the clearing house $220 and the clearing house pays Al $220.
   c. Al pays the clearing house $172 and the clearing house pays Bob $174.2.
   d. None; no payments are made until July.

5. The current level of Standard & Poor's Index is 250. The prospective dividend yield is 3.2 percent, and the interest rate is 7 percent. What is the value of a one-year future on the index? (Assume all dividend payments occur at the end of the year.)
    a. 230.7
    b. 250.0
*   c. 259.5
    d. 267.5
    e. Can't say without knowing the outlook for the market.

6. Refer back to the previous question. Suppose that the next day investors revise their forecast of dividends up by 10 percent and that the S&P Index also rises by 10 percent. What is the likely change in the price of the one-year future?
    a. Less than 10 percent because the futures price is higher than the spot price.
*   b. 10 percent.
    c. More than 10 percent because futures offer leverage.
    d. Need more information to solve.

7. Suppose that over a 6-month period, the price of gold is unchanged at $500 an ounce. If you bought 1-year gold futures at the beginning of the period, how would the value of your investment change? Assume an interest rate of 10 percent a year.
*   a. It would rise in value by about 5 percent.
    b. It would rise by 10 percent in line with the interest rate.
    c. It would not change.
    d. Cannot say - it depends on other factors.

8. The spot price for delivery of home heating oil is $.550 per gallon. The futures price for one year from now is $.560. If the risk-free rate is 6 percent per year, what is the PV(net convenience yield)?
    a. $.041
    b. $.010
*   c. $.022
    d. $.044
    e. $.023

9. Suppose that the spot rate of exchange is $1 = 5 French francs. Suppose also that the 1-year interest rate is 7.5 percent for dollars and 9 percent for French francs. What is the 1-year forward rate of exchange between dollars and francs?
   a. $1 = 6.00 francs
   b. $1 = 5.86 francs
   c. $1 = 4.93 francs
* d. $1 = 5.07 francs

10. Square Peg has some outstanding fixed-rate Australian dollar debt, which it wishes to convert into fixed-rate yen debt. It can achieve this conversion:
* a. By a swap whereby it pays yen and receives Australian dollars.
   b. By a swap whereby it pays Australian dollars and receives yen.
   c. Neither (a) nor (b) will achieve the desired conversion.

11. Suppose that a firm is required to pay out $100,000 at the end of each of the next two years. If the interest rate is 10 percent, which of the following would hedge this liability?
* a. Invest $128,000 in a zero-coupon, 2-year bond and $45,600 in short-term (e.g., overnight) debt.
   b. Invest $147,600 in a zero-coupon, 2-year bond and $52,500 in short-term (e.g., overnight) debt.
   c. Invest $100,000 in a zero-coupon, 2-year bond and $100,000 in short-term (e.g., overnight) debt.
   d. None of the above.

12. A company should consider using derivatives whenever:
   a. The treasury department is a profit center.
   b. There is excess cash available for investment.
   c. The necessary management controls are in place.
* d. Hedging will reduce the company's risk.
   e. All of the above.

13. Forward contracts differ from futures contracts because:
   a. Forward contracts are standardized with respect to units; futures contracts are not standardized.
   b. Forward contracts are marked to market; futures contracts are not marked to market.
* c. Forward contracts do not trade on organized exchanges; futures contracts do trade on organized exchanges.
   d. All of the above.
   e. None of the above; forward contracts and futures contracts are essentially identical.

14. Suppose you borrow $95.24 for one year at 5% and invest $95.24 for two years at 7%. For the time period beginning one year from today, you have:
    a. Borrowed at 7%.
    b. Invested at 7%.
    c. Borrowed at 9%.
    * d. Invested at 9%.
    e. None of the above.

15. Suppose you borrow $94.34 for two years at 8% and invest $94.34 for one year at 6%. For the time period beginning one year from today, you have:
    * a. Borrowed at 10%.
    b. Invested at 10%.
    c. Borrowed at 8%.
    d. Invested at 8%.
    e. None of the above.

16. A cable manufacturer estimates that a $100 rise in the price of a ton of copper on average knocks $5,000 off the value of the company, and vice versa. If the company is currently valued at $5 million, how can it hedge against fluctuations in the copper price?
    a. By selling futures on 50 tons of copper.
    * b. By buying futures on 50 tons of copper.
    c. By selling futures on 1000 tons of copper.
    d. By buying spot 50,000 tons of copper.
    e. It cannot - this risk cannot be hedged.

17. Suppose six-month stock index futures trade at 505 when the index is 500. The six-month interest rate is 3%, and the average dividend yield of stocks is 4% per year. Is there an arbitrage opportunity here?
    a. Yes.
    * b. No.
    c. It depends on market conditions.

18. Suppose six-month stock index futures trade at 410 when the index is 400. The six-month interest rate is 4%, and the average dividend yield of stocks is 6% per year. Is there an arbitrage opportunity here?
    * a. Yes.
    b. No.
    c. It depends on market conditions.

19. First National Bank has made a 5-year, $100 million fixed-rate loan at 10 percent. Annual interest payments are $10 million, and all principal will be repaid in year 5. The bank wants to swap the fixed interest payments into a floating-rate annuity. If the bank could borrow at a fixed rate of 8 percent for 5 years, what is the notional principal of the swap?
    a. $ 80 million.
    b. $100 million.
*   c. $125 million.
    d. $180 million.
    e. None of the above.

20. Third National Bank has made a 10-year, $25 million fixed-rate loan at 12 percent. Annual interest payments are $3 million, and all principal will be repaid in year 10. The bank wants to swap the fixed interest payments into a floating-rate annuity. If the bank could borrow at a fixed rate of 10 percent for 10 years, what is the notional principal of the swap?
    a. $40 million.
    b. $20 million.
    c. $25 million.
*   d. $30 million.
    e. None of the above.

Chapter 25 - True-False Questions

F   1. Because hedging is at best a zero-Net Present Value transaction, there is no valid economic reason for firms to hedge.

T   2. "Moral hazard" refers to situations where the insured, because he is insured, is less careful to take proper precautions against damage.

F   3. "Adverse selection" refers to the insurance industry practice of refusing to insure high-risk operations.

T   4. A futures contract is an example of a derivative security.

F   5. For a financial future, it is always true that the present value of the future price, calculated at the risk-free rate of interest, is equal to the spot price.

T   6. "Mark to market" means that each day any profits or losses are calculated and your account adjusted accordingly.

F   7. A cotton farmer can protect himself against a decline in cotton prices by buying cotton futures before the harvest.

T   8. Instead of buying guilders one-year forward, a U.S. company could issue a one-year dollar loan, change the receipts into guilders in the spot market and lend the guilders for one year. The two strategies have the same result.

F   9. For financial futures,

$$\frac{\text{Spot price}}{(1 + r_f)^t} = \text{Futures price} - \text{PV(dividends or interest foregone)}$$

T   10. Convenience yield is the extra value created by holding the actual commodity rather than a financial claim on it.

F   11. For commodity futures,

$$\frac{\text{Futures price}}{(1 + r_f)^t} = \text{Spot price} - \text{PV(Storage costs)} + \text{PV(Convenience yield)}$$

T   12. A company that wishes to lock in an interest rate on future borrowing can either enter into a forward rate agreement or it can borrow long-term funds and lend short-term.

F   13. Some commodities such as pork bellies are very expensive to store. This reduces the value of the futures contract.

T   14. If you buy or sell a futures contract, you settle up the gains or losses each day. If you enter into a forward contract, no payments occur until the contract matures.

F   15. A 6-month forward rate agreement obligates the company to borrow a specified amount from the bank in 6 months' time. The interest rate is fixed, however.

T   16. In an interest rate swap, one firm generally pays a fixed stream of payments and receives a stream of payments that vary with the level of short-term interest rates. No cash flows of principal are usually exchanged.

F   17. Basis risk is that risk caused by different methods used to place a value, or basis, on a hedge position.

T   18. The hedge ratio, or delta, measures the sensitivity of the value of one asset relative to the value of another asset.

F   19. A company that uses derivatives is speculating.

T   20. In order to set up a dynamic hedge to immunize against changes in interest rates, the asset and the liability must have the same present value and duration.

Chapter 25 - Essay Questions

1. Discuss the circumstances under which a company should consider self-insurance.

<u>Answer</u>

A company should consider self-insurance whenever - from the perspective of the insurance company - the administrative costs, the costs of adverse selection, or the moral hazard costs of obtaining the insurance are high. In these situations, buying insurance will not be a zero-NPV transaction, and there may be attractive alternatives, including self-insurance.

2. Are companies which trade in derivative securities speculating?

<u>Answer</u>

No. Whether a company is speculating or insuring or hedging, all of which may be done with derivatives, depends on the circumstances of the company. That is, it all depends on the risks the company is exposed to and whether the activity in derivatives serves to reduce or increase such risk.

Chapter 26 - Multiple Choice Questions

1. Which of the following statements is *not* true?
    a. The lessee does not have to buy the equipment.
    b. The lessee is responsible for making the lease payments.
  * c. The lease payments are not tax-deductible.
    d. The lessee gives up the depreciation tax shield.
    e. All of the above.

2. Which of the following are dubious reasons for leasing?
  * a. Leasing avoids capital expenditure controls.
    b. Tax shields can be used.
    c. The lessor is well equipped to provide efficient maintenance.
    d. Standardization leads to low administrative and transaction costs.
    e. All of the above.

3. Which of the following are dubious reasons for leasing?
    a. Short-term leases are convenient.
    b. The lessor is better able to assess or bear the risks of obsolescence.
    c. Leasing is cheaper.
  * d. Leasing improves book rate of return.
    e. All of the above.

4. The Financial Accounting Standards Board requires that all capital leases be capitalized. Which of the following qualify as capital leases?
    a. The lease lasts for at least 50 percent of the asset's estimated economic life.
  * b. The lessee can purchase the asset for a bargain price when the lease expires.
    c. The lease agreement transfers ownership to the lessee when the lease expires.
    d. The present value of lease payments is 75 percent of asset value.
    e. None of the above.

5. The Financial Accounting Standards Board requires that all capital leases be capitalized. Which of the following qualify as capital leases?
    a. The lease lasts for less than 50 percent of the asset's estimated economic life.
    b. The lessee can purchase the asset for fair market value when the lease expires.
*   c. The lease agreement transfers ownership to the lessee before the lease expires.
    d. The present value of lease payments is 75 percent of asset value.
    e. None of the above.

6. Which of the following conditions in a lease agreement would probably cause the Internal Revenue Service to treat the lease as an installment sale?
    a. Giving the lessee the right to acquire the assets for $1 when the lease expires.
    b. Limiting the lessee's right to issue debt while the lease is in force.
    c. Limiting the lessee's right to pay dividends while the lease is in force.
    d. Designating part of the lease payment as interest.
*   e. All of the above.

7. Assume the initial financing provided by a lease is $100,000 and the present value of the cash outflow attributable to the lease is $90,000. Then the net value of the lease is:
*   a. $10,000
    b. -$10,000
    c. $190,000
    d. None of the above.

8. Assume the initial financing provided by a lease is $200,000 and the present value of the cash outflow attributable to the lease is $180,000. Then the net value of the lease is:
    a. $380,000
    b. -$20,000
*   c. $20,000
    d. None of the above.

9. Assume the initial financing provided by a lease is $100,000 and the present value of the cash outflow attributable to the lease is $115,000. Then the net value of the lease is:
    a. $15,000
*   b. -$15,000
    c. $215,000
    d. None of the above.

10. Assume the initial financing provided by a lease is $500,000 and the present value of the cash outflow attributable to the lease is $525,000. Then the net value of the lease is:
* a. -$25,000
   b. $25,000
   c. $1,025,000
   d. None of the above.

11. Let LP_t equal the lease payment in year t, T_c equal the corporate tax rate, and DEP_t equal depreciation in year t. What is the lessee's net lease cash outflow in year t?
   a. $(1 - T_c)LP_t - T_c DEP_t$
   b. $(1 - T_c)LP_t$
   c. $T_c LP_t + (1 - T_c)DEP_t$
* d. $(1 - T_c)LP_t + T_c DEP_t$

12. If the interest rate on debt is r_D, what adjusted discount rate should the company use when valuing financial leases? The marginal tax rate is T_c.
* a. $r_D(1 - T_c)$
   b. $r_D T_c$
   c. r_D
   d. $1 - r_D T_c$
   e. None of the above.

13. Which of the following changes would make leasing more attractive? Assume the lessee is not paying taxes.
   a. A fall in interest rates.
   b. A reduction in the leased asset's expected economic life.
   c. A general decrease in the corporate tax rate.
* d. A switch from straight-line to accelerated tax depreciation.
   e. None of the above.

14. Which of the following changes would make leasing more attractive? Assume the lessee is not paying taxes.
   a. A fall in interest rates.
   b. A reduction in the leased asset's expected economic life.
* c. A general increase in the corporate tax rate.
   d. A switch from accelerated to straight-line to tax depreciation.
   e. None of the above.

15. A computer costs $500,000 and is depreciated for tax purposes straight-line over years 1 through 5. Assume that it has zero salvage value at the end of 5 years. The user wishes to lease the computer by making 5 annual lease payments, the first of which is due immediately. If taxes are paid without delay and the rate of interest is 10 percent, what is the minimum acceptable lease payment for a lessor who pays tax at 35 percent?
    a. $123,000
*   b. $136,000
    c. $146,000
    d. $200,000
    e. Need more information to solve.

16. A truck costs $50,000 and is depreciated for tax purposes straight-line over years 1 through 4. Assume that it has zero salvage value at the end of 4 years. The user wishes to lease the computer by making 4 annual lease payments, the first of which is due immediately. If taxes are paid without delay and the rate of interest is 8 percent, what is the minimum acceptable lease payment for a lessor who pays tax at 35 percent?
    a. $10,000
    b. $15,000
    c. $12,000
*   d. $13,000
    e. Need more information to solve.

17. A printing press costs $200,000 and is depreciated for tax purposes straight-line over years 1 through 8. Assume that it has zero salvage value at the end of 8 years. The user wishes to lease the computer by making 8 annual lease payments, the first of which is due immediately. If taxes are paid without delay and the rate of interest is 12 percent, what is the minimum acceptable lease payment for a lessor who pays tax at 35 percent?
    a. $60,000
*   b. $57,000
    c. $53,000
    d. $50,000
    e. Need more information to solve.

18. Assume a lessor establishes lease payments by charging that amount necessary to ensure its (i.e., the lessor's) net present value is zero. Other things equal, as the lessor's tax rate increases, the value of the lease to the lessee will:
*   a. Increase.
    b. Decrease.
    c. Remain the same.
    d. Need more information to solve.

19. Assume a lessor establishes lease payments by charging that amount necessary to ensure its (i.e., the lessor's) net present value is zero. Other things equal, as the lessor moves from straight-line to accelerated depreciation, the value of the lease to the lessee will:
     a. Remain the same.
     b. Decrease.
*   c. Increase.
     d. Need more information to solve.

20. Assume a lessor establishes lease payments by charging that amount necessary to ensure its (i.e., the lessor's) net present value is zero. Other things equal, as the length of the lease decreases, the value of the lease to the lessee will:
     a. Remain the same.
     b. Increase.
     c. Need more information to solve.
*   d. Decrease.

Chapter 26 - True-False Questions

T   1.   The user of the leased asset is called the lessee; the owner is called the lessor.

F   2.   A rental agreement that extends for six months or more and involves a series of fixed payments is called a lease.

T   3.   When a full-payout lease expires, the leased equipment is handed over to the lessor.

F   4.   A short-term, cancelable lease is known as a financial lease; a long-term, non-cancelable lease is called an operating lease.

T   5.   Under a net lease, the lessee agrees to maintain and insure the equipment and pay any property taxes.

F   6.   Under a leveraged lease, the lessee borrows money; this money is then used to make the lease payment.

T   7.   Financial leases are a source of financing.

F   8.   Since 1976 long-term leases do not need to be shown on the firm's balance sheet.

T   9.   If a company only wants use of an asset for a short period, it is often cheaper and more convenient to lease it. Such a lease is an operating lease.

F   10. Leasing is more likely to be advantageous if the tax rate of the lessor is low relative to that of the lessee.

T   11. Long-term lease obligations should be considered equivalent to debt.

F   12. A lease which lasts for at least 50% of an asset's estimated economic life is a capital lease.

T   13. Operating leases pass the risk of obsolescence from the user to the lessor.

F   14. Leasing is more likely to be advantageous when interest rates are low.

T   15. Sometimes the lessee can purchase the leased asset for a nominal amount, e.g., $1, when the lease expires. Such a lease would most likely be treated as an installment sale for tax purposes.

F   16.   Leasing is more likely to be advantageous when the lease period is short.

T   17.   To evaluate a lease one can compare the financing provided by the lease with the financing provided by an equivalent loan - that is, a loan which commits the firm to exactly the same cash outflows as the lease.

F   18.   A financial lease is superior to buying and borrowing if the financing provided by the lease is less than the financing generated by the equivalent loan.

T   19.   Leasing is more likely to be advantageous when depreciation is accelerated.

F   20.   Other things equal, higher nominal interest rates should increase the level of lease payments and therefore decrease the volume of financial leasing transactions.

T   21.   Financial leases can be evaluated by discounting lease cash flows at the company's after-tax borrowing rate.

Chapter 26 - Essay Questions

1. Discuss the differences between an operating lease and a financial lease.

Answer

Operating leases are short-term in nature and may be cancelled by the lessee during the life of the lease. Financing leases are long-term, extending over most of the estimated economic life of the asset, and cannot be cancelled (or perhaps can be cancelled if a substantial penalty is paid to the lessor).

2. Discuss the conditions under which leasing may be advantageous.

Answer

There are several conditions which result in a leasing arrangement being in the best interests of both the lessee and the lessor. However, the critical condition is that the lessor's tax rate is substantially higher than that of the lessee. If this is not the case, there is no advantage to leasing. On the other hand, if the tax rates do differ, leasing allows the transfer of tax shields to the company which can make the better use of them. Other conditions which increase the value of the lease to both lessee and lessor occur when the depreciation tax shield is received early in the lease period, when the lease period is long and the lease payments are concentrated toward the end of the lease period, and when the interest rate is high.

Chapter 27 - Multiple Choice Questions

The following information is necessary to answer problems 1-9:

Financial Statements for Snake Oil Company

Balance Sheets	1994	1995
Current Assets		
Cash	$ 8	$12
Receivables	20	24
Inventory	16	14
Fixed Assets		
Gross investment	50	60
Less depreciation	35	40
Net fixed assets	15	20
TOTAL Assets	$59	$70
Current liabilities		
Bank loans	5	3
Payables	18	20
Long-term debt	16	18
Net worth	20	29
TOTAL Liabilities and Net Worth	$59	$70
Stock price, per share:		$75

Income Statement	1995
Sales	$300
Cost of goods sold	270
Gross profit	30
Interest	1
Tax	12
Net income	$ 17
Dividend	$ 3

1. Snake Oil's Payout Ratio is:
   a. 56.7%
   b. 10.0%
 * c. 17.6%
   d. 1.0%
   e. 16.7%

2. Snake Oil's Average Collection Period is:
 * a. 26.8
   b. 25.7
   c. 23.1
   d. 20.0
   e. 35.6

3. Snake Oil's Inventory Turnover is:
   a. 20.3
   b. 25.7
   c. 15.5
 * d. 18.0
   e. 16.0

4. Snake Oil's Return On Equity is:
   a. 85.0%
   b. 15.0%
   c. 12.2%
   d. 58.6%
 * e. 69.4%

5. Snake Oil's Times Interest Earned is:
   a. 12
 * b. 30
   c. 17
   d. 3
   e. .54

6. Snake Oil's Current Ratio (1995) is:
 * a. 2.2
   b. .6
   c. 1.6
   d. 1.7
   e. 2.4

7. Snake Oil's Quick Ratio (1995) is:
   a. 2.2
   b. .6
 * c. 1.6
   d. 1.7
   e. 2.4

8. Snake Oil's Dividend Yield is:
   a. 15.0%
   b. 17.6%
   c. 5.1%
   d. 4.3%
 * e. 4.0%

9. Snake Oil's P/E Ratio is:
   a. 4.1
   b. 25.0
   c. 4.4
   d. 2.5
 * e. Need more information to solve.

10. Which of these ratios is a measure of liquidity?
   a. Tobin's q.
 * b. Quick ratio.
   c. Average collection period.
   d. Times interest earned.
   e. None of the above.

11. Which of these ratios is a measure of liquidity?
   a. Tobin's q.
   b. Average collection period.
   c. Times interest earned.
 * d. Interval measure.
   e. None of the above.

12. A high P/E ratio could indicate that:
   a. Tobin's q is low.
   b. The investors require a high return.
 * c. The company is expected to achieve average growth while paying out a higher than average proportion of earnings.
   d. Earnings are temporarily high.
   e. None of the above.

13. A high P/E ratio could indicate that:
 * a. Investors expect high dividend growth.
   b. The investors require a high return.
   c. The stock market is in a slump.
   d. Earnings are temporarily high.
   e. None of the above.

14. Which of these statements characterizes Tobin's q?
   a. The numerator is the market value of the firm's equity.
 * b. The assets in the denominator are measured at current, net replacement cost.
   c. Firms have an incentive to invest when q is less than 1.
   d. Firms with a strong competitive advantage tend to have a low q.
   e. None of the above.

15. Which of these statements characterizes Tobin's q?
   a. The numerator is the market value of the firm's equity.
   b. Firms have an incentive to invest when q is less than 1.
   c. Firms with a strong competitive advantage tend to have a low q.
* d. The denominator includes all assets, not just the firm's net worth.
   e. None of the above.

16. Which measure would be most useful in comparing the operating profitability of two firms in different industries?

   a. Net profit margin = $\dfrac{\text{EBIT} - \text{tax}}{\text{sales}}$

   b. Return on equity = $\dfrac{\text{Net earnings}}{\text{Average book equity}}$

   c. Sales to total assets = $\dfrac{\text{Sales}}{\text{Average book assets}}$

   d. Earnings to assets = $\dfrac{\text{Net earnings}}{\text{Average book assets}}$

* e. Return on assets = $\dfrac{\text{EBIT} - \text{tax}}{\text{Average book assets}}$

17. Which of these statements correctly describes earnings?
   a. Accountants try to measure economic earnings.
* b. Economic earnings follow a random walk (to a first approximation).
   c. Economic earnings cannot be negative.
   d. Accounting earnings fluctuate more than economic earnings.
   e. None of the above.

18. Which of these statements correctly describe(s) earnings?
* a. Accountants seldom capitalize investment in intangible assets. Therefore, true income is understated when a firm makes a large investment in an intangible asset.
    b. Economic earnings cannot be negative.
    c. Accounting earnings fluctuate more than economic earnings.
    d. Accounting earnings cannot be negative.
    e. None of the above.

19. Financial ratios may be used to estimate:
    a. The market risk of equity.
    b. A company's bond ratings.
* c. Both a and b.
    d. None of the above.

20. Inflation affects reported earnings in a variety of ways, including:
    a. Generating inventory profits.
    b. Understating depreciation.
    c. Neither a nor b.
* d. Both a and b.

Chapter 27 - True-False Questions

T   1.   Ratios can help you to ask the right questions; they rarely answer these questions.

F   2.   A company's debt-equity ratio is lower than its debt ratio.

T   3.   If you are using the return on assets to compare the operating performance of different firms, it makes sense to adjust income by adding back the interest tax shields.

F   4.   A high inventory turnover is always a sign of efficiency.

T   5.   The interval measure records the number of days the firm can finance operations out of its current liquid assets.

F   6.   The return on assets equals net income after interest and taxes divided by net book assets.

T   7.   Growth in equity from plowback equals:
$(1 - \text{payout ratio}) \cdot \text{return on equity}$

F   8.   Return on assets equals:
sales-to-assets ratio · sales-to-income ratio

T   9.   Under certain conditions, a firm's price-earnings ratio may be infinite.

F   10. The current ratio is lower than the quick ratio.

T   11. A high value of Tobin's q usually means there are valuable growth opportunities.

F   12. Tobin's q equals the ratio of stock price to book value per share for firms that do not borrow.

T   13. For most companies, the percentage of changes in net income due to industry influences is greater than the percentage of changes in net income due to economy-wide influences.

F   14. Since reported earnings follow roughly a random walk, one can do little better than assume that next year's earnings will lie on the long-term trend.

T   15. Accountants seem more interested in showing the long-run average profitability of a firm's assets than in tracking year-to-year economic income.

F   16. The SEC has issued guidelines requiring nine common financial ratios to be included in public companies' annual reports.

T   17. "Inventory profit" is defined to be that part of the profit from a sale of goods which can be attributed to the inflation which occurred while the goods were held by the company.

F   18. Financial ratios cannot be used to predict bond ratings with any degree of accuracy.

T   19. In inflationary periods, lenders demand a higher interest rate to compensate for the prospective decline in the real value of their loan. Book income recognizes the cost to the firm of the higher interest payment but not the benefit of the decline in the real value of the debt.

F   20. "Accounting beta" is simply another term for the market beta of a common stock.

T   21. As inflation progresses, the net book value of fixed assets becomes more and more out of date. Book depreciation understates real depreciation, and book income is overstated.

Chapter 27 - Essay Questions

1. Discuss some of the accounting issues that must be considered when interpreting a firm's financial ratios.

Answer
A complete answer will include most of the following:

Depreciation - firm's policies on depreciation will vary, and this will affect reported earnings.

Deferred taxes - considered by many to be a deferred liability, but considered by others to be really equity because these taxes (for an on-going concern) will never be paid.

Intangible assets - many firms generate considerable value through spending on intangible assets such as research and development.

Goodwill - the precise meaning and value of goodwill are hard to interpret, and so firms that carry a substantial amount of goodwill on their balance sheets are difficult to compare to those that do not.

Off-balance sheet items - short-term leases, for example, are off-balance sheet items that may reflect a considerable commitment for some firms, similar to debt. Other such items are derivative securities (e.g., swaps).

Pensions - under-funded pensions generate a liability that must be shown on the balance sheet; over-funded pension funds generate an asset that cannot be shown on the balance sheet.

2. Discuss the uses of financial ratios.

Answer
Financial ratios can be used to evaluate a company relative to its historical performance and thereby gain some idea of how the company's performance has changed over time. Such comparisons can also be made between a company and the industry as a whole, so as to gain some understanding of how this particular company differs from what is typical within its industry.

Financial ratios can also be used to estimate market risk, which is useful in situations where there is no direct measure (i.e., no traded common stock); and to predict bond ratings, which is useful because the yield on a bond is closely tied to its rating.

Chapter 28 - Multiple Choice Questions

1. Financial planning is necessary because:
   a. Financing and investment decisions interact.
   b. It helps to avoid financial surprises.
   c. It provides standards for measuring performance.
* d. All of the above.
   e. None of the above.

2. Financial planning is necessary because:
   a. Capital budgeting methods treat projects like a black box.
   b. The CEO must incorporate the performance goals established by the Human Resources Department.
   c. Financial models should be tested in the real world.
   d. All of the above.
* e. None of the above.

3. Which of the following would be included in a typical financial plan?
* a. Forecasted dividends.
   b. Year-by-year forecasts of the firm's stock price.
   c. Detailed lists of planned expenditures for capital equipment - machines, trucks, computers, etc.
   d. a and c.
   e. All of the above.

4. Which of the following would be included in a typical financial plan?
   a. A summary of planned financing.
   b. *Pro forma* balance sheets and income statements.
   c. Planned capital expenditures by division or line of business.
   d. A narrative description of business strategies for reaching the company's financial goals.
* e. All of the above.

5. A firm with financial slack is characterized by:
   a. Limited operating cash flow.
   b. Low dividend payout.
* c. Limited investment opportunities.
   d. All of the above.
   e. None of the above.

216

6. A firm with financial slack is characterized by:
* a. Moderate dividend payout.
   b. Low dividend payout.
   c. Limited operating cash flow.
   d. All of the above.
   e. None of the above.

7. Which of the following events is a symptom of poor financial planning?
   a. A firm stops paying cash dividends after a sudden drop in sales and profits.
   b. Antipollution regulations force a foundry to close. It could have continued operating if it had invested in pollution control equipment.
   c. A manufacturer passes up a lucrative contract because of a lack of production capacity.
   d. All of the above.
* e. Need more information to say.

8. Corporate financing models typically do not incorporate:
   a. Financial statements.
* b. Incremental cash flow.
   c. Market share forecasts.
   d. All of the above.
   e. None of the above.

9. Corporate financing models typically do not incorporate:
   a. Financial statements.
   b. Sales forecasts.
* c. Net present value.
   d. All of the above.
   e. None of the above.

10. Which of the following statements is true?
* a. Corporate financial models are usually based on accounting concepts.
   b. Corporate financial models usually calculate the NPV of the firm's investment plan.
   c. Corporate financial models usually calculate the firm's optimal debt ratio.
   d. All of the above.
   e. None of the above.

USE THE FOLLOWING INFORMATION TO ANSWER QUESTIONS 11-13.

At the beginning of 1996, R. Nocerus Inc. had the following balance sheet:

Net working capital	$30	$40	Debt
Fixed assets	70	60	Equity
	$100	$100	

Profits during 1996 were as follows:

Gross profit	$40
Interest (@ 10%)	4
Pretax profit	36
Tax	18
Net profit	$18
Dividend	$ 6
Retained earnings	$12

The company makes no deductions for depreciation, and the corporate income tax rate is 35 percent. The company expects to continue to earn 40 percent on start-of-year assets.

11. If the company keeps to a one-third payout ratio and raises no external finance, what is the forecast for end-of-year (i.e., at the end of 1996 or the beginning of 1997) total assets?
    a. $118
    b. $ 94
*   c. $112
    d. $100
    e. $106

12. If the company keeps to a one-third payout ratio and raises no external finance, what is the expected net profit in 1997?
    a. $18.0
*   b. $29.1
    c. $15.7
    d. $44.8
    e. $25.2

13. If the company forecasts an increase in sales of 25 percent for 1996, how much external financing will be required, assuming the productivity of assets remains unchanged?
    a. None
    b. $25
    c. $19
*   d. $13
    e. $15

14. The firm's internal growth rate is defined as:
    a. The average internal rate of return on its investments.
*   b. The ratio of retained earnings to total assets.
    c. Return on equity times the ratio of equity to total assets.
    d. Earnings available for common divided by equity.
    e. None of the above.

15. A firm can achieve a higher growth rate without raising external capital by:
    a. Increasing the proportion of debt in its capital structure.
    b. Decreasing its inventory turnover.
    c. Increasing its current ratio.
*   d. Increasing its plowback ratio.
    e. None of the above.

16. The sustainable growth rate is equal to:
*   a. The plowback ratio times the return on equity.
    b. The return on equity divided by the plowback ratio.
    c. The return on assets times the plowback ratio.
    d. The plowback ratio times the return on equity times the ratio of equity to assets.
    e. None of the above.

17. Last year Axle Inc. reported total assets of $200, equity of $70, net income of $50, dividends of $10 and retained earnings of $40. What is Axle Inc.'s internal growth rate?
    a. 25.0%
    b. 57.1%
*   c. 20.0%
    d. 71.4%
    e. 10.0%

18. Last year Axle Inc. reported total assets of $200, equity of $70, net income of $50, dividends of $10 and retained earnings of $40. What is Axle Inc.'s sustainable growth rate?
    a. 25.0%
*   b. 57.1%
    c. 20.0%
    d. 71.4%
    e. 10.0%

19. Last year Foley Inc. reported total assets of $500, equity of $400, net income of $120, dividends of $70 and retained earnings of $50. What is Foley Inc.'s internal growth rate?
   a. 24.0%
   b. 17.5%
   c. 30.0%
* d. 10.0%
   e. 12.5%

20. Last year Foley Inc. reported total assets of $500, equity of $400, net income of $120, dividends of $70 and retained earnings of $50. What is Foley Inc.'s sustainable growth rate?
   a. 24.0%
   b. 17.5%
   c. 30.0%
   d. 10.0%
* e. 12.5%

Chapter 28 - True-False Questions

F   1. Financial planning attempts to minimize risk.

T   2. Financial planning is necessary because investment and financing decisions interact.

F   3. Financial planning is concerned with the most likely outcome.

T   4. Strategic planning involves capital budgeting on a grand scale.

F   5. "Financial slack" refers to a firm that has no formal financial planning process.

T   6. One way to think of financial planning is that it is the management of the portfolio of real options held by the firm.

F   7. Covenants on existing bonds are irrelevant in the financial planning process, although they are of great concern in the day-to-day management of the firm.

T   8. Financial planning is less necessary for a firm with financial slack than for a firm that has few liquid assets and has borrowed up to the limit.

F   9. Good financial planning models incorporate considerable detail about future investment and financing decisions.

T   10. The financial plan will usually include *pro forma* balance sheets, income statements, and sources and uses of cash statements.

F   11. The financial planning process focuses on the most likely outcomes.

T   12. Financial planning does not attempt to minimize the risks the firm is exposed to.

F   13. Simulation models that are used in financial planning calculate the best financial strategy for the firm.

T   14. Most corporate financial models are simulation models designed to project the financial consequences of alternative financial strategies.

F   15. The internal growth rate is defined as the maximum company growth rate which is achievable for a constant level of the company's profit margin.

T   16.   The process of financial planning forces managers to be consistent in their goals for growth, investment, and financing.

F   17.   For any particular company, its internal growth rate is less than or equal to its sustainable growth rate.

T   18.   The internal growth rate is defined as the maximum rate at which a company can grow while financing all its needs for capital from earnings.

F   19.   The sustainable growth rate is the highest growth rate achievable by the firm over a ten-year time horizon.

T   20.   The internal growth rate is equal to the product of three things: the plowback ratio, the return on equity, and the ratio of equity to assets.

F   21.   For most companies, the sustainable growth rate is equal to the internal growth rate.

T   22.   The sustainable growth rate is the highest growth rate the firm can maintain without increasing its financial leverage.

Chapter 28 - Essay Questions

1. Discuss the elements of the financial planning process.

Answer

The key elements of the financial planning process that should be discussed are:
- Analyzing the financing and investment choices facing the firm;
- Projecting the future consequences of possible decisions;
- Deciding which alternatives should be chosen; and
- Measuring subsequent performance against the goals established in the financial plan.

2. Discuss the role of accounting information in financial planning.

Answer

Accounting information is crucial in the financial planning process; for example, one key element of the financial plan is *pro forma* financial statements. However, one must not stop with the analysis and production of accounting information: Other critical elements include things not easily captured by accounting information, such as net present value, the distinction between market risk and unique risk, and the cost of equity capital.

Chapter 29 - Multiple Choice Questions

1. The cost of holding inventory includes:
   a. Storage costs.
   b. Risk of spoilage.
   c. Risk of obsolescence.
   d. Opportunity cost of capital.
   * e. All of the above.

2. Which of the following is a source of cash?
   * a. Reduction in inventory.
   b. Increase in receivables.
   c. Purchase of marketable securities.
   d. Investment in fixed assets.
   e. None of the above.

3. Which of the following is a source of cash?
   a. Increase in receivables.
   b. Purchase of marketable securities.
   * c. Increase in payables.
   d. Investment in fixed assets.
   e. None of the above.

4. Which of the following is a source of cash?
   a. Payment of dividend.
   * b. Depreciation.
   c. Investment in fixed assets.
   d. Repayment of bank loan.
   e. None of the above.

5. Which of the following is a use of funds?
   a. Decrease in inventory.
   b. Sale of marketable securities.
   c. Issue of common stock.
   * d. Payment of dividends.
   e. None of the above.

6. Which of the following is a use of funds?
   a. Increase in payables.
   b. Sale of marketable securities.
   * c. Investment in fixed assets.
   d. Issue of common stock.
   e. None of the above.

7. Cash flow is different from "net income plus depreciation" because:
   a. Depreciation is an expense.
 * b. Not all sales are cash sales.
   c. Of taxes.
   d. A and B.
   e. The statement is wrong; cash flow is the same as "net income plus depreciation".

8. Preparing a cash budget is important because:
   a. It provides an early warning system with respect to future shortages of cash.
   b. It provides a standard against which future performance can be judged.
   c. It is an essential first step in preparing a sources and uses of cash statement.
   d. All of the above.
 * e. A and B.

9. A company has forecast sales in the first 3 months of the year as follows (figures in millions):

January	February	March
$60	$80	$100

Sixty percent of sales are usually paid for in the month that they take place and 40 percent in the following month. Receivables at the end of December were $24 million. What are the forecasted collections on accounts receivable in March?
   a. $88 million.
 * b. $92 million.
   c. $100 million.
   d. $140 million.
   e. None of the above.

10. A company has forecast sales in the first 3 months of the year as follows (figures in millions):

January	February	March
$90	$20	$30

Seventy percent of sales are usually paid for in the month that they take place and 30 percent in the following month. Receivables at the end of December were $20 million. What are the forecasted collections on accounts receivable in March?
 * a. $27 million.
   b. $50 million.
   c. $23 million.
   d. $35 million.
   e. None of the above.

11. A company has forecast sales in the first 3 months of the year as follows (figures in millions):

January	February	March
$80	$60	$40

Seventy percent of sales are usually paid for in the month that they take place, 20 percent in the following month, and the final 10 percent in the next month. Receivables at the end of December were $23 million. What are the forecasted collections on accounts receivable in March?
    a. $180 million.
    b. $13 million.
    c. $40 million.
*   d. $48 million.
    e. None of the above.

12. A company has forecast sales in the first 3 months of the year as follows (figures in millions):

January	February	March
$200	$140	$100

Fifty percent of sales are usually paid for in the month that they take place, 30 percent in the following month, and the final 20 percent in the next month. Receivables at the end of December were $100 million. What are the forecasted collections on accounts receivable in March?
*   a. $132 million.
    b. $100 million.
    c. $240 million.
    d. $92 million.
    e. None of the above.

13. A company has forecast sales in the first 3 months of the year as follows (figures in millions):

January	February	March
$200	$140	$100

Fifty percent of sales are usually paid for in the month that they take place, 30 percent in the following month, and the final 20 percent in the next month. Receivables at the end of December were $100 million. What is the forecast for outstanding receivables at the end of March?
    a. $132 million.
    b. $100 million.
*   c. $78 million.
    d. $92 million.
    e. Need more information to solve.

USE THE FOLLOWING FINANCIAL STATEMENTS OF SNAKE OIL CO. TO ANSWER
QUESTIONS 14 AND 15.

Balance Sheets	1995	1996
Current Assets		
Cash	$ 8	$12
Inventory	16	14
Receivables	20	24
Fixed Assets		
Gross investment	50	60
Less depreciation	35	40
Net fixed assets	15	20
TOTAL Assets	$59	$70
Current Liabilities		
Bank loans	5	3
Payables	18	20
Long-term debt	16	18
Net worth	20	29
TOTAL Liabilities and Net Worth	$59	$70

Income Statement	1996
Sales	$300
Cost of goods sold	270
Gross profit	30
Interest	1
Tax	12
Net income	$ 12
Dividend	$ 3

14. The total sources of cash are:
    a. $ 4
    b. $12
  * c. $23
    d. $30
    e. None of the above.

15. The total sources of funds are:
    a. $ 4
    b. $12
  * c. $19
    d. $23
    e. None of the above.

USE THE FOLLOWING FINANCIAL STATEMENTS OF EKANS OIL CO. TO ANSWER
QUESTIONS 16 AND 17.

Balance Sheets	1995	1996
Current Assets		
Cash	$ 9	$15
Inventory	19	13
Receivables	25	27
Fixed Assets		
Gross investment	70	80
Less depreciation	45	50
Net fixed assets	25	30
TOTAL Assets	$78	$85
Current Liabilities		
Bank loans	10	15
Payables	22	10
Long-term debt	15	25
Net worth	31	35
TOTAL Liabilities and Net Worth	$78	$85

Income Statement	1996
Sales	$280
Cost of goods sold	250
Gross profit	30
Interest	1
Tax	11
Net income	$ 18
Dividend	$ 14

16. The total sources of cash are:
    a. $ 4
    b. $33
    c. $18
  * d. $44
    e. None of the above.

17. The total sources of funds are:
    a. $ 4
  * b. $33
    c. $18
    d. $44
    e. None of the above.

228

18. A company has forecast sales in the first 3 months of the year as follows (figures in millions):

January	February	March
$70	$60	$80

Sixty percent of sales are usually paid for in the month that they take place, 30 percent in the following month, and the final 10 percent in the next month. Receivables at the end of December were $40 million. What is the forecast for outstanding receivables at the end of March?
- a. $32 million.
- b. $140 million.
- c. $73 million.
- * d. $38 million.
- e. Need more information to solve.

19. Common sources of short-term financing include:
- * a. Stretching payables.
- b. Issuing bonds.
- c. Reducing inventory.
- d. All of the above.
- e. None of the above.

20. Firms that borrow from commercial banks may:
- a. Pay a rate less than the Treasury bill rate.
- * b. Be required to keep a compensating balance at the bank.
- c. Be required to stretch their payables.
- d. All of the above.
- e. None of the above.

Chapter 29 - True-False Questions

F 1. Net working capital is the total of the firm's current assets and current liabilities.

T 2. One cost of holding inventory is the opportunity cost of capital.

F 3. The principal current asset is accounts payable.

T 4. The cumulative capital requirement of the firm may be met with either short-term or long-term financing.

F 5. The best level of long-term financing relative to the firm's cumulative capital requirement may be found by using a linear programming model.

T 6. Most financial managers attempt to "match maturities" of assets and liabilities. That is, they tend to finance long-lived assets with long-term borrowing or equity.

F 7. Firms with excess cash are able to invest in marketable securities and thereby increase shareholder wealth.

T 8. Most firms make a permanent investment in net working capital.

F 9. By definition, all investment in working capital is short-term.

T 10. A firm with excess cash can at best generate a zero NPV from investing it in marketable securities.

F 11. Sources of cash include the issue of long-term debt, reduction of inventory, increases in accounts payable, and purchases of marketable securities.

T 12. Uses of cash include payment of cash dividends, repayment of loans, investment in plant and equipment, and increases in accounts receivable.

F 13. Depreciation is not included in sources of cash because it is an expense.

T 14. When goods are sold, inventories are converted to accounts receivable and, when customers pay their bills, the accounts receivable are converted to cash. There is only one constant in this process - namely, working capital.

F 15. Cash flow may be defined as "net income plus depreciation".

T   16. Sources and uses of funds statements trace changes in net working capital.

F   17. Ending accounts receivable = beginning accounts receivable - sales + collections

T   18. If the bank requires compensating balances, the firm needs to borrow more than its forecasted cash requirements.

F   19. Stretching payables is always a good deal because there is no cost to not paying your bills on time.

T   20. Two common sources of short-term financing are borrowing from a bank and stretching payables.

F   21. Commercial finance companies offer loans at rates comparable to those of banks but do not require collateral.

Chapter 29 - Essay Questions

1. Discuss the reasons why a company should prepare a cash budget.

Answer

There are two primary reasons why the preparation of a cash budget is essential. First, cash holds a very special place in our economy: It is the only asset that may be used to pay bills. Thus, running short of cash is a serious problem and should be avoided. Preparing a cash budget helps the manager forecast cash inflows and cash outflows and hence forecast when and how much external financing will be needed. Second, the cash budget, once developed, provides a benchmark against which future performance may be measured. This is useful to make sure that the overall management of cash within the company is proceeding as anticipated.

2. Discuss the process of preparing s short-term financial plan.

Answer

We start with the cash budget, which shows the firm's anticipated cash inflows and outflows over the relevant planning horizon. Then we add in possible sources of financing - bank loans, stretching payables, loans from a commercial finance company, etc., along with estimates of their costs. Doing this we come up with an estimate of total cash required each time period along with where that cash is going to come from. Then the plan is discussed and evaluated and if necessary, changed; thus the final plan is developed through a process of trial and error. Smaller companies use spreadsheet packages on personal computers to do this; larger companies may actually have a formal, mathematical model which is used.

Chapter 30 - Multiple Choice Questions

1. Generally a seller will require faster payment if its customers:
    a. Are in low-risk businesses.
    b. Have large accounts.
  * c. Quickly resell the goods.
    d. All of the above.
    e. None of the above.

2. Suppose you purchase goods on terms of 10/20, net 60. Taking compounding into account, what annual rate of interest is implied by the cash discount? (Assume a year has 365 days.)
    a. 91 percent.
    b. 139 percent.
    c. 250 percent.
  * d. 162 percent.
    e. 182 percent.

3. Suppose you purchase goods on terms of 5/10, net 30. Taking compounding into account, what annual rate of interest is implied by the cash discount? (Assume a year has 365 days.)
  * a. 155 percent.
    b. 5 percent.
    c. 91 percent.
    d. 255 percent.
    e. 144 percent.

4. Suppose you purchase goods on terms of 2/10, net 50. Taking compounding into account, what annual rate of interest is implied by the cash discount? (Assume a year has 365 days.)
    a. 2 percent.
  * b. 20 percent.
    c. 102 percent.
    d. 18 percent.
    e. 73 percent.

5. Which of the following transactions involve credit?
    a. COD.
  * b. 2/30, net 60.
    c. Payment-on-sight draft in exchange for shipping document.
    d. CBD.
    e. None of the above.

6. Which of the following does not involve credit?
   a. Payment on time draft.
   b. 2/10, net 30.
   c. Open account.
   d. Promissory note.
   * e. None of the above.

7. Sources of information regarding a company's creditworthiness include:
   a. Dun & Bradstreet.
   b. Its financial statements.
   c. Moody's.
   * d. All of the above.
   e. None of the above.

8. A customer has ordered goods with a value of $800. The production cost is $600. Under what conditions should you extend credit if there is no possibility of repeat orders?
   a. If the probability of payment exceeds .67.
   * b. If the probability of payment exceeds .75.
   c. If the probability of payment exceeds .80.
   d. If the probability of payment exceeds .90.
   e. Should always extend credit - price exceeds the cost.

9. A customer has ordered goods with a value of $1200. The production cost is $800. Under what conditions should you extend credit if there is no possibility of repeat orders?
   * a. If the probability of payment exceeds .67.
   b. If the probability of payment exceeds .75.
   c. If the probability of payment exceeds .80.
   d. If the probability of payment exceeds .90.
   e. Should always extend credit - price exceeds the cost.

10. A customer has ordered goods with a value of $2000. The production cost is $1800. Under what conditions should you extend credit if there is no possibility of repeat orders?
    a. If the probability of payment exceeds .67.
    b. If the probability of payment exceeds .75.
    c. If the probability of payment exceeds .80.
    * d. If the probability of payment exceeds .90.
    e. Should always extend credit - price exceeds the cost.

11. Which of the following statements is true?
    a. Companies should focus on the immediate order, not on possible future orders that are uncertain.
    b. Companies should concentrate their credit analysis on small and doubtful orders.
    * c. Companies with low profit margins need to be particularly careful about extending credit to high-risk customers.
    d. All of the above.
    e. None of the above.

12. Which of the following statements is true?
    * a. New companies must be prepared to incur more bad debts than established businesses as part of the cost of building up a good customer list.
    b. To ensure fairness, companies should give each customer the same type of credit analysis.
    c. Companies with high profit margins need to be particularly careful about extending credit to high-risk customers.
    d. All of the above.
    e. None of the above.

13. Which of the following statements is true?
    a. Bank acceptances are seldom used in overseas trade.
    b. A time draft is another name for a sight draft.
    * c. An irrevocable letter of credit ensures that funds are available to pay the bill.
    d. Weak customers often default on commercial drafts.
    e. None of the above.

14. Which of the following statements is true?
    * a. Promissory notes eliminate the possibility of subsequent disputes about the existence of debt.
    b. Bank acceptances are seldom used in overseas trade.
    c. A conditional sale is a common practice in the U.S.
    d. Weak customers often default on sight drafts.
    e. None of the above.

15. A firm has annual sales of $365 million. Currently, customers take an average of 60 days to pay. If the collection period can be permanently reduced by one day and the cost of capital is 10 percent, what is the increase in company value?
    a. Zero.
    b. $100,000.
    c. $500,000.
    * d. $1 million.

16. The default rate of Demurrage Associates' new customers has been running at 10 percent. The average sale for each new customer amounts to $800, generating a profit of $100 and a 40 percent chance of a repeat order next year. The default rate on repeat orders is only 2 percent. If the interest rate is 9 percent, what is the expected profit from each new customer?
     a. $ 88.70
     b. $ 47.75
     c. $101.00
     d. $ 43.25
*   e. $ 50.83

17. The default rate of Don's new customers has been running at 20 percent. The average sale for each new customer amounts to $500, generating a profit of $200 and a 30 percent chance of a repeat order next year. The default rate on repeat orders is only 5 percent. If the interest rate is 6 percent, what is the expected profit from each new customer?
     a. $152.50
*   b. $149.53
     c. $275.00
     d. $100.00
     e. $175.00

18. Tom's Toys is currently experiencing a bad debt ratio of 6 percent. Tom is convinced that, with tighter credit controls, he can reduce this ratio to 2 percent; however, he expects sales to drop by 8 percent as a result. The cost of goods sold is 75 percent of the selling price. Per $100 of current sales, what is Tom's expected profit under the proposed credit standards?
     a. $15.2
     b. $23.0
     c. $19.0
     d. $27.0
*   e. $21.2

19. Terry's Place is currently experiencing a bad debt ratio of 4 percent. Terry is convinced that, with looser credit controls, this ratio will increase to 8 percent; however, she expects sales to increase by 10 percent as a result. The cost of goods sold is 80 percent of the selling price. Per $100 of current sales, what is Terry's expected profit under the proposed credit standards?
     a. $26.0
     b. $15.4
*   c. $13.2
     d. $25.6
     e. $18.0

20. Toni's Catering is currently experiencing a bad debt ratio of 5 percent. Terry is convinced that, with looser credit controls, this ratio will increase to 10 percent; however, she expects sales to increase by 20 percent as a result. The cost of goods sold is 90 percent of the selling price. Per $100 of current sales, what is Toni's expected profit under the proposed credit standards?
* a. $0
  b. $12
  c. $10
  d. $ 5
  e. $13

Chapter 30 - True-False Questions

F   1. Generally a seller will allow longer credit if the customer is in a high-risk business.

T   2. Generally a seller will allow longer credit if the goods are not quickly resold.

F   3. If a firm sells goods on terms of 2/30 net 60, customers who do not take the cash discount are effectively borrowing money at an approximate rate of 2 percent per year.

T   4. If a firm sells goods on terms of 2/30 net 60, customers who pay within 30 days are entitled to a 2 percent discount. Otherwise they must pay in full within 60 days.

F   5. If goods are sold on open account, the customer is asked to sign a formal IOU.

T   6. A commercial draft is simply an order to pay.

F   7. If a commercial draft is an order to pay immediately, it is called a time draft.

T   8. In a conditional sale, the title of the goods remains with the seller until full payment is made.

F   9. One source of credit information is Dann and Broadstreet.

T   10. Although firms are not allowed to discriminate between customers, firms are allowed to offer different credit terms to different classes of buyers.

F   11. Credit scoring makes sense when a company has a few large customers.

T   12. Multiple discriminant analysis is a statistical technique that can be used to discriminate between good and bad credit risks.

F   13. The credit manager's job is to minimize the number of bad accounts.

T   14. Companies with high profit margins can afford to grant credit to riskier customers.

F   15. It is never worth accepting a relatively poor credit risk.

T   16. It is important to concentrate credit analysis on the large and dangerous accounts.

F   17. Credit insurance companies are often called "factors."

T   18. A factor buys the firm's receivables, and the customer then makes payment direct to the factor.

F   19. Dun and Bradstreet is probably the best-known factoring company.

T   20. The FCIA insures export credits.

Chapter 30 - Essay Questions

1. Discuss the problems associated with using a single measure such as "average age of the receivables" to monitor the efficiency of collection.

Answer
 Efficiency of account collection is not the only factor that affects the average age: A changing sales pattern will also have a strong influence. For example, a sharp increase in sales automatically reduces the *proportion* of past sales overdue and hence will reduce the average age of the receivables. Conversely, if there is a sharp fall in sales, a relatively high proportion of the amount owed may well be overdue, and the average age will increase.

2. Discuss the general principles that should guide the credit decision.

Answer
 In general, there are three principles of credit management. First, the overall goal of the credit decision process is the same as the goal of the firm: maximize shareholder wealth. In other words, the goal is neither to minimize bad debt expense nor to maximize sales. Second, the credit manager must focus on the dangerous accounts, typically the large ones. Here, an extensive credit investigation is usually time and money well-spent. Third, the credit manager must always look beyond the immediate order; that is, the credit manager must be sensitive to the long-run possibilities this customer offers.

Chapter 31 - Multiple Choice Questions

1. Baumol's model of cash balances states that Q is the square root of:

$$\frac{2(\text{Annual cash disbursements})(\text{Cost per sale of Treasury bills})}{\text{annual interest rate}}$$

What is Q?
   a. The number of times per annum bills should be sold.
   b. The average holding of bills.
 * c. The amount of bills that should be sold at any one time.
   d. The minimum holding of cash.
   e. None of the above.

2. Suppose that the interest rate on Treasury bills is 6 percent, and every sale of bills costs $60. You pay out cash at a rate of $800,000 a year. According to Baumol's model of cash balances, how many times a year should you sell bills?
 * a. 20
   b. 35
   c. 50
   d. 15
   e. 10

3. Suppose that the interest rate on Treasury bills is 6 percent, and every sale of bills costs $60. You pay out cash at a rate of $800,000 a year. According to Baumol's model of cash balances, what is Q?
   a. $17,376
   b. $20,000
   c. $10,000
   d. $50,000
 * e. $40,000

4. Suppose that the interest rate on Treasury bills is 4 percent, and every sale of bills costs $40. You pay out cash at a rate of $1,000,000 a quarter. According to Baumol's model of cash balances, how many times a quarter should you sell bills?
   a. 20
   b. 22
   c. 12
 * d. 11
   e. 29

5. Suppose that the annual interest rate on Treasury bills is 4 percent, and every sale of bills costs $40. You pay out cash at a rate of $1,000,000 a quarter. According to Baumol's model of cash balances, what is Q?
    a. $45,000
*   b. $90,000
    c. $35,000
    d. $85,000
    e. $50,000

6. Suppose that the interest rate on Treasury bills is 6 percent, and every sale of bills costs $20. You pay out cash at a rate of $400,000 a month. According to Baumol's model of cash balances, how many times a month should you sell bills?
    a. 63
    b. 23
*   c. 18
    d. 42
    e. 32

7. Suppose that the interest rate on Treasury bills is 6 percent, and every sale of bills costs $20. You pay out cash at a rate of $400,000 a month. According to Baumol's model of cash balances, what is Q?
    a. $16,000
    b. $24,000
    c. $31,000
    d. $43,000
*   e. $57,000

8. The Miller-Orr model predicts that the firm should sell or buy securities when the cash balance hits a lower or upper limit. How far should the cash balance be adjusted?
    a. Half-way between the upper and lower limits.
*   b. Closer to the lower limit.
    c. Closer to the upper limit.
    d. Right to the lower limit if the cash balance hits the upper limit; right to the upper limit if the cash balance hits the lower limit.

9. We should expect cash balances to increase when:
    a. Interest rates increase.
    b. Sales volume falls.
    c. The transaction costs of buying or selling interest-bearing securities decrease.
*   d. Uncertainty about day-to-day or week-to-week cash flows increases.
    e. None of the above.

10. We should expect cash balances to increase when:
* a. The transaction costs of buying or selling interest-bearing securities increase.
   b. Interest rates increase.
   c. Sales volume falls.
   d. Uncertainty about day-to-day or week-to-week cash flows decreases.
   e. None of the above.

11. Assume the minimum cash balance required is $20,000; the variance of daily cash flows is 5,000,000; the daily interest rate is .02 percent (i.e., .0002); and the transaction cost for each sale or purchase is $25. According to the Miller-Orr model, the spread between the lower and upper cash balance limits is:
   a. $ 5,000
   b. $27,400
   c. $15,600
   d. $31,700
* e. $23,300

12. Assume the minimum cash balance required is $10,000; the variance of daily cash flows is 2,000,000; the daily interest rate is .01 percent (i.e., .0001); and the transaction cost for each sale or purchase is $15. According to the Miller-Orr model, the spread between the lower and return cash balance limits is:
* a. $ 6,100
   b. $ 9,500
   c. $18,000
   d. $17,200
   e. $ 4,700

13. A large firm may hold substantial cash balances because:
   a. These balances are required by the bank.
   b. The company may have accounts in many different banks.
   c. The company may have a very decentralized organization.
* d. All of the above.
   e. None of the above.

14. If a company changes its payment procedures so that it takes its checks longer to be returned to its bank for payment, the company has decreased its:
   a. Payment float.
   b. Availability float.
   c. Net float.
   d. All of the above.
* e. None of the above.

15. Which of the following is a way for companies to speed up collections?
    a. Remote disbursing.
  * b. Concentration banking.
    c. Miller-Orr model.
    d. All of the above.
    e. None of the above.

16. General Chemicals is considering opening a lock box in Dogsville on October 1. The company expects that on average, 30 checks with a total value of $2,000 will be cleared through the lock box every day (i.e., a total of $730,000 a year). The bank charges $.05 for each check cleared through the lock box during the previous quarter. If the lock box makes cash available to the company two days earlier and the interest rate is 12 percent per year, what is the net present value (as of October 1) of the lock box? Assume each month has 30 days.
  * a. -$500
    b. $400
    c. $2,000
    d. $4,000
    e. $700

17. H. Pottamus, Inc., has $2 million on deposit with the bank. It now writes checks for $100,000 and $200,000 and deposits a check for $80,000. Two weeks later it learns that the $200,000 check and $80,000 check have cleared. What is the company's net float?
    a. $300,000
    b. $220,000
  * c. $100,000
    d. -$100,000
    e. None of the above.

18. Electronic cash transfers offer several advantages, including:
    a. A low marginal transactions cost.
    b. A reduced float.
    c. Easy automation of record-keeping.
  * d. All of the above.
    e. None of the above.

19. Which of the following is used to control disbursements?
    a. Concentration banking.
*   b. Zero-balance account.
    c. Lock-box system.
    d. Fedwire.
    e. None of the above.

20. Assume that the average number of daily payments to a lock-box is 200, the average size of the payment is $1,000, the rate of interest per day is .02 percent (i.e., .0002), the savings in mail time is 2 days, and the savings in processing time is 1 day. What is the daily return from operating the lock-box?
    a. $ 80
    b. $100
*   c. $120
    d. $130
    e. $140

Chapter 31 - True-False Questions

F   1. No rational manager would ever hold cash because no interest is earned on it.

T   2. One good reason to hold cash is that cash provides more liquidity than securities.

F   3. The marginal value of liquidity increases as you hold increasing amounts of cash.

T   4. Rational financial managers hold cash balances up to the point at which the marginal value of the interest foregone is equal to the marginal value of the liquidity gained.

F   5. If the interest rate is high, the firm should hold a relatively large cash balance.

T   6. The carrying cost of inventory includes the cost of the capital tied up as well as the cost of shelf or storage space.

F   7. It is impossible for a firm to hold too little cash.

T   8. For a firm with a steady stream of orders, as the average order size increases, the number of orders falls but the average inventory rises.

F   9. If there are large fluctuations in the firm's cash flows or if there are large costs to selling securities, the firm should hold relatively small average cash balances.

T   10. In the Miller-Orr model of cash management, the return point is one-third of the distance from the lower limit to the upper limit.

F   11. If the cost of cash balances (in terms of interest foregone) is 6 percent and the cost of borrowing is 8 percent, the cash manager should adjust the cash balances so that the probability that the firm will need to borrow is 2 percent.

T   12. For large firms, purchasing securities for even one day generally makes sense, even with transactions costs.

F   13. You can decrease your net collected cash balance by increasing your net float.

T   14. Concentration banking works as follows. The firm arranges for its customers to pay their bills directly to branch offices, which then deposit the checks into a local bank account. Any surplus funds are periodically transferred to a principal bank account.

F   15.   Concentration banking and lock-boxes are two ways companies use to increase their payment float.

T   16.   Sometimes companies ask customers to send their payments to a post office box, which is then emptied by the local bank.

F   17.   Electronic transfers of cash lead to an increase in float.

T   18.   Firms can pay for bank services by maintaining interest-free demand deposits.

F   19.   CHIPS is a controlled disbursement system used by major corporations.

T   20.   Fedwire is a system that can be used to transfer money between banks.

F   21.   The purpose of a zero-balance account is to speed collections.

Chapter 31 - Essay Questions

1. Discuss the primary trade-off involved in cash management.

Answer
The primary trade-off is between holding cash, which provides liquidity but no (or less) interest, and holding securities, which provide interest but less liquidity. This trade-off is incorporated into models of cash management, which - under fairly restrictive conditions - yield optimal solutions; two examples are the Baumol model under certainty and the Miller-Orr model under uncertainty.

2. Discuss the concept of float.

Answer
When a company writes a check, it decreases the ledger account labelled "checking." However, the actual amount of money in the bank will not decrease until the check has been received by the other party, deposited in its bank, and presented for payment. This difference between what is in the bank and what the company has on its books is called "payment float." Similarly, when a company receives a check, it is deposited (and the ledger amount increased), but the funds are not made available by the bank until several days later; this is called "availability float." The difference between these two is "net float." One goal of cash management is to increase a company's net float.

Chapter 32 - Multiple Choice Questions

1. The discount on a 91-Treasury bill is 5.2 percent. What is the annually compounded rate of return?
   - a. 4.80 percent.
   - b. 5.20 percent.
   - c. 5.27 percent.
   - * d. 5.45 percent.
   - e. 6.01 percent.

2. The discount on a 91-Treasury bill is 5.65 percent. What is the annually compounded rate of return?
   - a. 5.25 percent.
   - * b. 5.94 percent.
   - c. 5.65 percent.
   - d. 5.53 percent.
   - e. 1.45 percent.

3. The discount on a 91-Treasury bill is 4.83 percent. What is the annually compounded rate of return?
   - a. 4.83 percent.
   - b. 4.78 percent.
   - c. 1.22 percent.
   - d. 5.13 percent.
   - * e. 4.98 percent.

4. The three money market securities with the greatest volume of business are:
   - * a. Treasury bills, commercial paper, repurchase agreements.
   - b. Negotiable CDs, federal agency discount notes, T-bills.
   - c. Commercial paper, bankers' acceptances, tax-exempt municipal notes.
   - d. Federal agency discount notes, repurchase agreements, medium-term notes.
   - e. T-bills, federal agency discount notes, tax-exempt municipal notes.

5. For which of the following investments is there a very active secondary market?
   - a. Medium-term notes.
   - b. Commercial paper.
   - * c. US Treasury bills.
   - d. Repurchase agreements.
   - e. None of the above.

6. A repurchase agreement occurs when:
   a. A company agrees to buy back its commercial paper before maturity.
   b. A bank depositor agrees, in advance, to re-invest money in a negotiable certificate of deposit.
   * c. An investor buys part of a government security dealer's inventory and simultaneously agrees to sell it back.
   d. The federal government agrees to buy T-bills.
   e. A bank accepts a demand to pay a certain amount in the future.

7. A variable rate demand bond:
   a. Is a long-term security.
   b. Has interest payments linked to the level of short-term interest rates.
   c. May periodically be sold back to the issuer at face value.
   d. Is tax-exempt.
   * e. All of the above.

8. A tax-paying corporation would prefer to invest short-term money in:
   a. Preferred stock.
   * b. Floating-rate preferred stock.
   c. Common stock.
   d. Long-term bonds.
   e. None of the above.

9. If the short-term commercial paper rate is 10 percent and the corporate tax rate is 35 percent, what yield would a corporation require on an investment in floating-rate preferred stock? Assume the default risk is the same as for commercial paper.
   a. 15.2 percent.
   b. 10.0 percent.
   * c. 7.3 percent.
   d. 6.6 percent.
   e. 5.7 percent.

10. If the short-term commercial paper rate is 6 percent and the corporate tax rate is 35 percent, what yield would a corporation require on an investment in floating-rate preferred stock? Assume the default risk is the same as for commercial paper.
    a. 6.0 percent.
    b. 3.9 percent.
    c. 9.2 percent.
    * d. 4.4 percent.
    e. 2.3 percent.

11. If the short-term commercial paper rate is 8 percent and the corporate tax rate is 35 percent, what yield would a corporation require on an investment in floating-rate preferred stock? Assume the default risk is the same as for commercial paper.
* a. 5.8 percent.
  b. 5.3 percent.
  c. 4.6 percent.
  d. 4.4 percent.
  e. 3.9 percent.

12. Which of the following describes short-term bank loans?
  a. Often secured by a factoring agent.
  b. Almost never secured by inventory.
* c. Often prearranged as a line of credit.
  d. Cannot be from an international bank because of Federal Reserve System regulations.
  e. None of the above.

13. Which of the following describes short-term bank loans?
* a. If unsecured, banks often require borrower to "clean up" the loan for 1 month in the year.
  b. Often secured by commercial paper.
  c. Almost never secured by accounts receivable.
  d. Cannot be from an international bank because Federal Reserve System regulations prohibit Eurodollar borrowing.
  e. None of the above.

14. Which of the following statements describes bank term loans?
  a. Typical maturity is between 1 and 2 years.
  b. Usually repaid in increasing amounts over the term of the loan.
  c. Interest rate is usually fixed.
* d. Borrower is often obliged to maintain compensating balance.
  e. None of the above.

15. Which of the following statements describes bank term loans?
  a. Typical maturity is between 2 and 4 years.
* b. Usually repaid in level amounts over the term of the loan.
  c. Interest rate is usually fixed.
  d. Borrower is often obliged to have the bank manage its corporate cash accounts.
  e. None of the above.

16. The bank offers you a term loan at 8 percent on condition that you maintain a 20 percent compensating balance. What is the effective rate of interest?
        a.   6.4 percent.
*   b. 10.0 percent.
        c. 18.0 percent.
        d.   8.0 percent.
        e. 12.3 percent.

17. The bank offers you a term loan at 10 percent on condition that you maintain a 10 percent compensating balance. What is the effective rate of interest?
        a.   9.0 percent.
        b. 10.0 percent.
        c. 13.7 percent.
*   d. 11.1 percent.
        e.   8.6 percent.

18. The bank offers you a term loan at 11 percent on condition that you maintain a 20 percent compensating balance. What is the effective rate of interest?
*   a. 13.8 percent.
        b. 11.0 percent.
        c.   9.7 percent.
        d.   8.8 percent.
        e.   7.6 percent.

19. A typical condition associated with the granting of a term loan to a small business is:
        a. Life insurance on the senior managers.
        b. Limits on officer salaries.
        c. Owner's personal guarantee of repayment.
*   d. All of the above.
        e. None of the above.

20. Loan sales by commercial banks may take the form of:
        a. Loan assignments.
        b. Loan participations.
        c. Loan syndications.
        d. A, B and C.
*   e. A and B.

Chapter 32 - True-False Questions

F   1. The market for short- and long-term investments is known as the money market.

T   2. Short-term debt is usually not as risky as long-term debt.

F   3. LIBOR is a type of money market security that is traded internationally.

T   4. If the discount on a Treasury bill is 10 percent, the yield is more than 10 percent.

F   5. Because Treasury bills are sold at a discount, the interest is subject to capital gains tax.

T   6. A dollar-denominated deposit in a bank in Singapore is known as an Asian dollar deposit.

F   7. Treasury bills are issued with maturities of one, two, and three months.

T   8. Noncompetitive bids for Treasury bills are filled at the average price of the successful competitive bids.

F   9. Most agency securities are backed with the full faith and credit of the U.S. government.

T   10. The interest on municipal securities is exempt from federal income tax.

F   11. Large, safe, and well-known companies can bypass the banking system by issuing their own short-term notes. These notes are known as certificates of deposit.

T   12. Some firms sell their own commercial paper directly; others do so through dealers.

F   13. Repurchase agreements typically have maturities of 3 to 6 months.

T   14. New issues of securities that mature within 270 days do not need to be registered with the Securities and Exchange Commission (SEC).

F   15. There is an active secondary market for commercial paper.

T   16. A banker's acceptance begins life as a written demand for the bank to pay a given sum at a future date.

F   17. Taking into account issue costs and the cost of a backup line of credit, commercial paper is generally more expensive than a bank loan.

T   18. A line of credit allows the company to borrow from the bank at any time up to an established limit.

F   19. Factoring is simply another name for lending against receivables.

T   20. Under a repurchase agreement, the investor buys Treasury securities from a government security dealer and simultaneously arranges to sell them back at a later date at a higher price.

F   21. Floating rate preferreds are generally issued by tax-paying corporations because they can deduct 80 percent of the dividend from pre-tax income.

T   22. The interest rate on a line of credit is usually tied to the bank's prime rate or to LIBOR.

F   23. A firm that borrows on the security of its receivables is, to all intents and purposes, factoring its receivables.

T   24. Bank term loans usually have maturities of between one and eight years and are repaid in installments.

F   25. Automobiles, television sets, dishwashers, and apples make good collateral for inventory loans.

T   26. Revolving credit agreements are relatively expensive compared to straight lines of credit.

F   27. A revolving credit is a short-term bank loan secured by inventory. The credit is renewed as the inventory "turns over" and is replenished by new production.

Chapter 32 - Essay Questions

1. Discuss collateral from the perspective of a commercial bank.

Answer
   The guiding principle for a bank is that it must get its money back, and collateral is one way to assure that this will happen, even in the event the firm's cash flow is inadequate to repay the loan. Thus, collateral must be something that is easily converted to cash at a fair value. Examples of good collateral include current accounts receivable from trustworthy customers and raw material inventory, if it consists of standard items. Items banks would not take as collateral include work-in-process inventory and specialized equipment with no secondary market.

2. Discuss the similarities and differences between line of credit and term loans.

Answer
   They are similar in that both are loans from a bank, but differ in some of the terms and conditions. Lines of credit are short-term (although they are frequently renewed), while term loans are long-term, up to 8 years. Lines of credit usually finance working capital needs and thus typically require the line to be "paid down" for at least 30 consecutive days per year; term loans have no such requirement. On both types of loan, the rate is usually a floating one, tied to prime or perhaps LIBOR. And on both, some restrictions are put on the company by the bank: Collateral may be required, limits may be established for officer salaries, the company may be required to maintain its debt ratio at a certain level, etc.

Chapter 33 - Multiple Choice Questions

1. Firm A has a value of $100 million, and B has a value of $70 million. Merging the two would allow a cost savings with a present value of $20 million. Firm A purchases B for $75 million. What is the gain from this merger?
   - a. $30 million.
   - *b. $20 million.
   - c. $15 million.
   - d. $10 million.
   - e. None of the above.

2. Firm A has a value of $100 million, and B has a value of $70 million. Merging the two would allow a cost savings with a present value of $20 million. Firm A purchases B for $75 million. What is the cost of this merger?
   - a. $30 million.
   - b. $20 million.
   - c. $15 million.
   - d. $10 million.
   - *e. None of the above.

3. Firm A has a value of $100 million, and B has a value of $70 million. Merging the two would allow a cost savings with a present value of $20 million. Firm A purchases B for $75 million. How much do firm A's shareholders gain from this merger?
   - a. $30 million.
   - b. $20 million.
   - *c. $15 million.
   - d. $10 million.
   - e. None of the above.

4. Firm A has a value of $200 million, and B has a value of $120 million. Merging the two would allow a cost savings with a present value of $30 million. Firm A purchases B for $130 million. What is the gain from this merger?
   - *a. $ 30 million.
   - b. $ 20 million.
   - c. $100 million.
   - d. $ 80 million.
   - e. None of the above.

5. Firm A has a value of $200 million, and B has a value of $120 million. Merging the two would allow a cost savings with a present value of $30 million. Firm A purchases B for $130 million. What is the cost of this merger?
   a. $30 million.
   b. $20 million.
   c. $15 million.
  * d. $10 million.
   e. None of the above.

6. Firm A has a value of $200 million, and B has a value of $120 million. Merging the two would allow a cost savings with a present value of $30 million. Firm A purchases B for $130 million. How much do firm A's shareholders gain from this merger?
   a. $30 million.
  * b. $20 million.
   c. $15 million.
   d. $10 million.
   e. None of the above.

7. Which of the following mergers would be considered a horizontal merger?
  * a. General Motors acquires Ford.
   b. Consolidated Edison acquires Westinghouse.
   c. Xerox acquires Boeing.
   d. None of the above.
   e. All of the above.

8. Which of the following mergers would be considered a conglomerate merger?
   a. General Motors acquires Ford.
   b. Consolidated Edison acquires Westinghouse.
  * c. Xerox acquires Boeing.
   d. None of the above.
   e. All of the above.

9. The value of most businesses depends upon:
   a. Equipment, machinery, etc.
   b. Buildings, real estate, etc.
   c. Patents, licenses, etc.
  * d. Employees.
   e. None of the above.

10. A sensible reason for two companies to merge is if the merger will allow:
    a. Economies of scale.
    b. Economies of vertical integration.
    c. Combination of complementary resources.
    d. Elimination of efficiencies.
  * e. All of the above.

11. Which of the following is not a sensible reason for merger?
    a. Economies of vertical integration.
  * b. Diversification.
    c. Elimination of efficiencies.
    d. Ability to use tax shields.
    e. None of the above.

12. Guildenstern Inc. and Rosencrantz Inc. have decided to merge. Both companies have debt outstanding and this debt will become a claim against the new firm. Other things equal, which of the following statements is true?
  * a. The total market value of the two companies' debt is increased because risk is reduced.
    b. The total market value of the two companies' equity is increased because risk is reduced.
    c. If Guildenstern is more highly levered than Rosencrantz, then, other things equal, Guildenstern's bondholders will lose from the merger.
    d. If Rosencrantz is less risky than Guildenstern, then, other things equal, Rosencrantz's bondholders will gain from the merger.
    e. None of the above.

13. Companies A and B are valued as follows:

	A	B
No. of shares	2000	1000
Earnings per share	$10	$10
Share price	$100	$50

Company A now acquires B by offering one (new) share of A for every two shares of B (that is, after the merger, there are 2500 shares of A outstanding). If investors are aware that there are no economic gains from the merger, what is the price-earnings ratio of A's stock after the merger?
    a. 7.5
  * b. 8.3
    c. 10.0
    d. 5.0
    e. 12.0

14. Look again at question 13. Suppose that the merger really does increase the value of the combined firms by $20,000 (i.e., $PV_{AB} - PV_A - PV_B = \$20,000$). What is the cost of the merger?
    a. Zero.
    b. $2,000.
    c. $8,000.
    * d. $4,000.
    e. None of the above.

15. Companies A and B are valued as follows:

	A	B
No. of shares	5000	2000
Earnings per share	$80	$10
Share price	$100	$20

    Company A now acquires B by offering one (new) share of A for every five shares of B (that is, after the merger, there are 5400 shares of A outstanding). If investors are aware that there are no economic gains from the merger, what is the price-earnings ratio of A's stock after the merger?
    a. 2.00
    b. 1.03
    c. 1.25
    d. 1.63
    * e. 1.29

16. Which of the following is not a major item of U.S. antitrust legislation?
    * a. Garn-St. Germain Act
    b. Sherman Act.
    c. Clayton Act.
    d. Hart-Scott-Rodino Act.
    e. Celler-Kefauver Act.

17. What are the tax consequences of a taxable merger?
    a. Selling shareholders can defer any capital gain until they sell their shares in the merged company.
    b. Depreciation tax shield is unchanged by merger.
    * c. Selling shareholders must recognize any capital gain.
    d. Depreciable value of assets will remain unchanged.
    e. All of the above.

18. An example of a shark-repellent charter amendment is:
    a. Supermajority.
    b. Waiting period.
    c. Poison pill.
    d. Staggered board.
    * e. All of the above.

19. Leveraged buy-outs almost always involve:
    a. AAA grade debt.
    b. Issuance of new shares of stock to many investors.
    c. The existing management team as new shareholders.
  * d. Junk grade debt.
    e. All of the above.

20. Merger activity in the U.S. seems to coincide with:
    a. High real interest rates.
  * b. High general levels of stock prices.
    c. Low real interest rates.
    d. Low general levels of stock prices.
    e. All of the above: there is simply no pattern.

Chapter 33 - True-False Questions

T   1.   A merger produces an economic gain only if the two firms are worth more together than apart.

F   2.   The gain from a merger may be defined as:
$$PV_{AB} - (PV_A - PV_B)$$

T   3.   If Firm A acquires Firm B for cash, then the cost of the merger is equal to the cash payment minus B's value as a separate entity.

F   4.   A horizontal merger is one in which the buyer expands forward in the direction of the ultimate consumer or backward toward the source of raw materials.

T   5.   A vertical merger is one in which the buyer expands forward in the direction of the ultimate consumer or backward toward the source of raw materials.

F   6.   Diversification is a sensible reason for two companies to merge.

T   7.   Firms that are badly managed are natural acquisition targets.

F   8.   By reducing the interest rate on borrowing, mergers produce economic gains.

T   9.   Two companies should consider a merger if they have complementary resources.

F   10.   A sensible reason for one company to buy another is if the result is a higher earnings per share.

T   11.   Firms with high price-earnings (P/E) ratios can increase earnings per share by issuing stock to acquire low P/E firms.

F   12.   The cost of a merger is independent of whether cash or stock is used.

T   13.   If Company B is acquired by an issue of shares, the cost of the merger is equal to the value of B's shareholders' investment in the new firm minus the value of B as a separate entity.

F   14.   The Clayton Act effectively requires an acquiring company to "go public" with its bid.

T   15. Antitrust law is enforced by both the Justice Department and the Federal Trade Commission.

F   16. In a tax-free acquisition, the selling stockholders are treated for tax purposes as having sold their shares.

T   17. In an efficient capital market, it makes no difference whether a merger is viewed as a purchase of assets or a pooling of interests.

F   18. The buying company will always prefer a taxable arrangement if the current values of depreciable assets are substantially larger than their depreciable values in the hands of the seller.

T   19. In a successful two-tier offer, control is gained in the first tender offer, and the remaining shares are bought out at a lower price.

F   20. Tender offers are socalled because they involve a friendly approach to the management of the selling company.

F   21. Usually, the stockholders of the acquiring firm gain from a merger, whereas the stockholders of the selling firm generally lose.

T   22. It appears that target companies capture most of the gains in hostile takeovers.

F   23. Sometimes companies that are threatened with takeover pay out large special dividends to keep the loyalty of existing shareholders. This is called greenmail.

T   24. The most common reason for spin-offs is that they improve efficiency.

F   25. LBOs are rarely financed with junk debt.

T   26. Most LBOs are driven by a mixture of motives, including increased tax shields, increased incentives (because of increased company leverage), and available free cash flow.

F   27. There have been three major episodes of intense merger activity: one at the turn of the century, another in the late 1940s, and still another in the mid-1970s.

Chapter 33 - Essay Questions

1. Discuss the difficulties associated with a typical merger.

Answer

The difficulties are many and are easily overlooked. They include integration of production processes, training the sales force to understand new products, and the integration of accounting systems. Perhaps the biggest difficulty, however, is in merging two corporate cultures. Beliefs about "the way things should be" are deep-seated and only change slowly. If not handled well, the resulting turmoil among the management team can cause irreparable damage to the firm.

2. Discuss takeover defenses.

Answer

The fundamental goal of takeover defenses is to raise the price an acquiring firm must pay to take over a firm. This is accomplished by making the acquisition so difficult that it must be accomplished at a price acceptable to the selling firm and its stockholders. Examples of such defensive tactics include the incorporation of charter amendments (such as the supermajority, wherein a large majority of shareholders is required to approve a merger) and legal challenges (such as charging the hostile suitor with violating antitrust or security laws). One possible effect of such defensive tactics is the entrenchment of the current management team, which may not be in the best interests of the stockholders.

Chapter 34 - Multiple Choice Questions

1. The spot lira/dollar exchange rate is 833 lira/$, and the spot lira/sterling exchange rate is 1965 lira/£. What is the spot dollar/sterling exchange rate?
   - a. $2.28/£
   - * b. $2.36/£
   - c. $2.06/£
   - d. $0.42/£
   - e. None of the above.

2. The spot drachma/dollar exchange rate is 241 drachma/$, and the spot drachma/sterling exchange rate is 376 drachma/£. What is the spot dollar/sterling exchange rate?
   - * a. $1.56/£
   - b. $0.64/£
   - c. $0.40/£
   - d. $1.65/£
   - e. None of the above.

3. The spot lira/dollar exchange rate is 833 lira/$. The 3-month forward rate is 862 lira/$. What is the lira's forward premium (or discount) on the dollar, expressed as an annual rate?
   - a. 4 percent discount.
   - b. 4 percent premium.
   - * c. 14 percent discount.
   - d. 14 percent premium.
   - e. None of the above.

4. Look again at question 3. If the annually compounded interest rate on 3-month dollar CDs is 9-1/2 percent, what would you expect the annually compounded interest rate to be on 3-month lira CDs?
   - a. 3.5 percent.
   - b. 5.3 percent.
   - * c. 13.3 percent.
   - d. 25.6 percent.
   - e. Need more information to solve.

5. The spot drachma/dollar exchange rate is 241 drachma/$. The 3-month forward rate is 248 drachma/$. What is the drachma's forward premium (or discount) on the dollar, expressed as an annual rate?
   - a. 3 percent premium.
   - b. 3 percent discount.
   - c. 12 percent premium.
   - * d. 12 percent discount.
   - e. None of the above.

6. Look again at question 5. If the annually compounded interest rate on 3-month dollar CDs is 6-1/2 percent, what would you expect the annually compounded interest rate to be on 3-month drachma CDs?
* a. 9.6 percent.
  b. 3.1 percent.
  c. 3.5 percent.
  d. 11.7 percent.
  e. Need more information to solve.

7. The expectations theory of forward rates implies that:
  a. The forward rate is determined by government's expectations.
* b. On average, the forward rate is equal to the future spot rate.
  c. The forward rate is determined by expectations of the future spot interest rate.
  d. The forward rate is equal to the future spot rate.
  e. None of the above.

8. Assume that both the law of one price and the expectations theory of forward rates hold. The spot rate for the Ruritanean doubloon is .455 doubloon/$, and the one-year forward rate is .476 doubloon/$. Suppose that next year's forecasted rate of inflation in Ruritania is now revised upward by 10 percent. How does this affect exchange rates?
  a. The current spot rate changes to .501 doubloon/$.
* b. The forward rate changes to .524 doubloon/$.
  c. Next year's expected spot rate changes to .501 doubloon/$.
  d. The forward rate changes to .501 doubloon/$.
  e. Need more information.

9. Assume that international capital markets are competitive and that the Fisher hypothesis holds. The one-year interest rate is approximately 10 percent in the USA and 5 percent in Switzerland. If the expected inflation rate is 10 percent in the USA, what is the expected inflation rate in Switzerland?
  a. 15 percent.
  b. 10 percent.
  c. 7 percent.
* d. 5 percent.
  e. None of the above.

10. The Wol Book Company, a U.S.-based firm, needs to pay out £500,000 in 6 months' time. Which of the following actions would protect Wol against exchange risk?
    a. Buy pounds in 6 months' time.
    b. Sell pounds 6 months forward.
*   c. Borrow dollars for 6 months, use them to buy pounds in the spot market, and lend those pounds for 6 months.
    d. Borrow dollars for 6 months, use them to buy pounds in the spot market, and sell those pounds 6 months forward.
    e. None of the above.

11. The cost of hedging foreign currency exposure is:
    a. Today's spot rate.
    b. The expected future spot rate.
    c. Today's forward rate.
    d. The expected future forward rate.
*   e. None of the above.

12. An American firm with an operating subsidiary in Lilliput believes that the Lilliputian guinea is overvalued. Insofar as they are permitted, which of the following actions would protect the firm against a depreciation of the guinea?
*   a. The subsidiary uses local bank borrowing rather than funds provided by the parent.
    b. The subsidiary invoices its customers in guineas rather than dollars.
    c. The subsidiary buys its supplies locally.
    d. The subsidiary takes longer to pay for components supplied by the parent.
    e. None of the above.

13. An American firm with an operating subsidiary in Maxitania believes that the Maxitanian yeldit is overvalued. Insofar as they are permitted, which of the following actions would protect the firm against a depreciation of the yeldit?
    a. The subsidiary invoices its customers in yeldits rather than dollars.
*   b. The parent increases the price of components supplied to the subsidiary.
    c. The subsidiary takes longer to pay for components supplied by the parent.
    d. The subsidiary buys supplies locally.
    e. None of the above.

14. Square Peg is evaluating a new investment in Germany. It will cost 10 million DM and is forecast to produce income (at today's prices) of 2 million DM a year for 10 years. You have the following additional information:

Spot exchange rate:	$1 = 2 DM
Dollar risk-free interest rate:	8 percent
Dollar required return on project:	15 percent
Forecasted US inflation:	6 percent
DM risk-free interest rate:	5 percent

What is the project's NPV?
* a. $ .7 million.
  b. $1.4 million.
  c. $1.6 million.
  d. $2.3 million.
  e. $3.1 million.

15. Look at question 14. If you wished to evaluate the project in nominal terms, what figure should you assume for the expected inflation rate in Germany?
  a. 2 percent.
  b. 6 percent.
  c. 7 percent.
* d. 3 percent.
  e. 5 percent.

16. Look at question 14. If you wished to discount the dollar cash flows from the project, what should you assume for the spot exchange rate in year 10?
  a. $1 = .75 DM
  b. $1 = 2.00 DM
* c. $1 = 1.52 DM
  d. $1 = 2.65 DM
  e. $1 = 3.58 DM

17. If the expectations theory of forward rates holds, then the cost of insuring against exchange rate losses (as a percent of the amount insured) is:
* a. Zero.
  b. Less than the domestic inflation rate.
  c. Greater than the domestic inflation rate.
  d. Equal to the domestic inflation rate.
  e. None of the above.

18. Hexagon Inc. is evaluating a new investment in France. It will cost 30 million francs and is forecast to produce income (at today's prices) of 12 million francs a year for 8 years. You have the following additional information:

    Spot exchange rate: $1 = 4.90 francs
    Dollar risk-free interest rate: 6 percent
    Dollar required return on project: 20 percent
    Forecasted US inflation: 3 percent
    Franc risk-free interest rate: 9 percent

What is the project's NPV?
    a. $ 4.7 million.
    b. $ 11.7 million.
    c. $ 3.3 million.
*   d. $ 2.4 million.
    e. $ 23.0 million.

19. Look at question 18. If you wished to evaluate the project in nominal terms, what figure should you assume for the expected inflation rate in France?
    a. 2 percent.
    b. 3 percent.
    c. 7 percent.
    d. 5 percent.
*   e. 6 percent.

20. Look at question 18. If you wished to discount the dollar cash flows from the project, what should you assume for the spot exchange rate in year 8?
*   a. $1 = 6.12 francs
    b. $1 = 2.58 francs
    c. $1 = 4.90 francs
    d. $1 = 7.63 francs
    e. $1 = 3.92 francs

Chapter 34 - True-False Questions

T 1. In the forward exchange market, currency is bought for future delivery.

F 2. The interest rate parity theory says that real interest rates must be the same worldwide.

T 3. If the dollar interest rate is higher than the guilder interest rate, then in equilibrium the dollar must trade at a forward discount.

F 4. If traders do not like risk, the dollar will generally stand at a forward discount.

T 5. The expectations theory of exchange rates states that the expected change in the spot rate is equal to the percentage difference between the forward rate and the spot rate.

F 6. In equilibrium, the interest rates in any two countries must be the same.

T 7. The law of one price implies that the change in the spot exchange rate equals the difference between the two countries' inflation rates.

F 8. The forward exchange rate is an accurate predictor of the future spot rate.

T 9. In equilibrium, the real interest rates in any two countries must be the same.

F 10. The law of one price holds for most countries.

T 11. On average, the forward rate is equal to the spot rate.

F 12. Large differences in inflation rates are rarely accompanied by offsetting changes in the exchange rate.

T 13. In the Eurocurrency market interest rate parity almost always holds.

F 14. The cost of hedging foreign currency risk is the difference between the forward rate and the spot rate.

T 15. The cost of hedging foreign currency risk is the difference between the forward rate and the expected spot rate.

F 16. Companies should direct their capital investment toward countries with strong currencies and away from those with weak currencies.

T   17.   A company that wishes to build a plant in a country whose currency appears to be overvalued can protect itself against loss by simultaneously borrowing in that country's currency.

F   18.   If investors can diversify more cheaply than corporations, corporations will have an incentive to expand overseas.

T   19.   If there is a 40 percent chance that your plant in Ruritania will be expropriated next year without compensation, the expected cash flows will be only 60 percent as high as if there were no such possibility.

F   20.   The terms "transaction exposure" and "economic exposure" are two names for the same thing - foreign exchange risk.

T   21.   Despite the apparent benefits to international diversification, most investors invest the bulk of their funds domestically. This could be because foreign investment involves additional costs.

F   22.   If a country has a double taxation agreement with the United States, then any U.S. company is taxed twice on any profits made overseas.

T   23.   Project financing is often designed to reduce a foreign government's incentive to expropriate fixed capital investment.

Chapter 34 - Essay Questions

1. Discuss the law of one price.

Answer
　　The law of one price states that the expected difference in inflation rates equals the expected change in the spot rate. For goods that are standard and easily and cheaply transported, this law will hold (as long as trade barriers do not exist). If this were not so, a profit opportunity would exist and those exploiting this opportunity would force prices to change such that this law would hold. For many goods, however, transportation costs are high, and so the law of one price does not hold, in general.

2. Discuss the method(s) companies should use when they make international capital expenditure decisions.

Answer
　　The general method remains the same - take all projects with a positive net present value. There are, however, two approaches to calculating net present value. The first step in each method is the same - estimate the cash flows in terms of the currency in whose country the project will be located. Then, using the first method, all these cash flows are converted to the company's home currency using spot and forward exchange rates and the net present value calculated. Using the second method, the net present value is first calculated in terms of the foreign currency, and this net present value is converted to the company's home currency using the spot rate.

-NOTES-

-NOTES-

NOTES

-NOTES-

-NOTES-